THE ONLY REAL ESTATE INVESTING FOR BEGINNERS BOOK YOU'LL EVER NEED

CLOSE YOUR FIRST DEAL IN 7 SIMPLE STEPS EVEN IF YOU'RE BROKE & HAVE ZERO EXPERIENCE

ANDREW & COURTNEY JAMES

PERMANENT
PTO
Spend Life Living

Published by Read Street Press LLC, Appleton, WI
Copyright © 2023 by Read Street Press LLC

DOWNLOAD THE AUDIOBOOK
VERSION FOR FREE

If you love listening to audiobooks on-the-go, you can download the audiobook version of this book for FREE (Regularly $14.95) just by signing up for a FREE 30-day audible trial!

Visit the link below to get started:
https://bit.ly/real-estate-bounty-us

CONTENTS

Part II

HOW TO CLOSE YOUR FIRST DEAL IN 7
SIMPLE STEPS

INTRODUCTION: WHY YOU ARE HERE

Do you crave freedom? Do you want the ability to do what you want, when you want, without worrying if you have enough money or if your boss will let you take time off work?

I know what you're going through because I've also been there, like many others. I used to dread clocking in not one minute later than 8 AM to my job, catching up on emails regarding problems I didn't actually care about, sitting in on what seemed like the same meeting over and over again, and waiting in agony for my coveted lunch hour. And even after this hour of freedom, I'd go back to my desk and watch the time tick by as slowly as possible as if it were mocking me and waiting for the most exciting part of my day, which was clocking out without any forced post-work gatherings to take up the rest of the evening. Then I'd peel out of the parking lot so I could complete a few necessary life tasks and, hopefully, still have time and energy at the end of the day to do something I enjoyed. But let's be honest. The day drained me so much that I usually ended up being too tired to do anything. Most of the time, I ended up cracking a few beers and watching Netflix before going to bed and doing it all over again.

If any of this resonates with you, you are reading the right book, and there is a way out. If you want to leave your 9-to-5 job and finally be free to pursue the life of your dreams, it IS possible!

Imagine being able to book a flight on a moment's notice in the middle of the week, take your spouse on a two-hour lunch date on a Tuesday, or spend the 40+ hours you usually work and commute with your kids without having to worry about making ends meet or upper management breathing down your neck. This lifestyle IS possible, even for the person who feels utterly stuck or far behind!

The best way to do this is by building passive income and generating wealth through real estate investing. I know this because I used to loathe my life as an employee. Now I am a full-time real estate and business investor living the life of my dreams, and I want to help you live yours.

So, if you want to dive into the world and endless possibilities of real estate investing, let's buckle up and get started!

PART I

THE POWER OF REAL ESTATE INVESTING

1

HOW REAL ESTATE INVESTING CAN MAKE ORDINARY PEOPLE EXTRAORDINARILY WEALTHY

The major fortunes in America have been made in land.

— JOHN D. ROCKEFELLER

Did you know that real estate investing has created 90% of the world's millionaires, and most started as beginners like you?

The secret is that regular people are getting richer than ever using real estate investing, and you can, too.

You might wonder, "If this is true, why don't more people invest in real estate?"

Well, there are many answers to that question. Some common reasons are that they don't think they can invest in real estate or know how to. However, the biggest reason seems to be that they believe they need tons of money, connections, or skills to get started.

The good news is this couldn't be further from the truth! Anyone can build a wealth-generating real estate portfolio with the correct knowledge and the drive to do so.

What is real estate investing anyway? Simply put, it's the purchase, management, or sale of real estate (homes, buildings, land, etc.) for a profit. There are many different types of real estate investments and just as many, if not more, ways to make money. This makes it a very flexible asset class to invest in that is also relatively easy to get started in. The average person can start with just one small investment and scale an extensive portfolio. They can do this relatively quickly or build it slowly over time, depending on their goals. The sky really is the limit!

So, how does real estate investing work? There are many ways that real estate investing can be done to generate wealth, but let's introduce the most common ways first.

To start, there's rental property investing. This is where someone buys a property, commonly with a down payment and a bank loan, and manages it while tenants rent it out and pay down the mortgage for them. Not only is the mortgage being paid down by other people, but hopefully, there is extra money left over from the rent payment after paying expenses to put in the investor's pocket every month. Most likely, the property is also increasing in value over time, making the investor even more of a return down the line. Imagine having 10s or 100s of these properties all operating at the same time! Probably the other most common way to build wealth through real estate is buying a property at or below its value, drastically renovating it to increase its value, and then selling it at a much higher price than what you bought it for and what you put into fixing it up.

These are just two high-level examples of hundreds of ways to build wealth through real estate investing. While real estate can significantly increase your wealth, this is not some "get rich quick" scheme; it can take several years. You have to come into the real estate business with the mindset that it's a long-term strategy. This often involves commitment, patience, and being hungry to learn anything you can about real estate to become a better investor.

Real estate investing has many other benefits beyond just wealth creation. Let's dive in to learn more!

THE SECRET SAUCE OF REAL ESTATE INVESTING

While there are many benefits to real estate investing, there are four key elements to amassing significant wealth. All four of them, working together, are what make real estate a unique and powerful investment.

These four elements are: tax benefits, appreciation, cash flow, and leverage. I like to refer to them as the secret sauce of real estate investing. Let's take a closer look at each.

UNDERSTANDING TAX BENEFITS

Let's begin with property tax deductions. I'm starting with these because these tend to be some of the most expensive taxes a real estate investor will have. However, they are often tax deductible, which means you can reduce them on your tax bill. Plus, if you already own your primary residence (the house you live in), you can deduct a part of your property taxes, too.

Another tax benefit is mortgage interest deduction, where you can deduct your mortgage interest payments. So, all the interest you pay on your mortgage can be taken out of your tax bill. This is great because, most of the time, you will be taking out mortgages to purchase your properties. It might not seem like much, but this is considerable savings, especially when you start your career as a real estate investor and when your interest payments are higher.

But perhaps one of the best tax benefits of real estate investing is depreciation. You can deduct the cost of acquiring a rental property over a certain period, which is usually 27.5 years or 39 years for residential and commercial property, respectively. This means that the depreciation expense can counterbalance your rental income, which reduces your tax bill.

Then there's the 1031 exchange, also called the tax-deferred exchange. This is more of a strategy where you can defer capital gains on a property when you sell if you use that money to invest in a similar property. The capital gains tax is a tax on the profit from the sale of real estate. For instance, if you sell a one-bedroom property and buy another one, any capital gains you've made with the sale can be deferred. This is a great way to continue to expand your real estate portfolio without a large tax bill. But more importantly, over a long period of time, the 1031 exchange can save you a lot of money.

Besides the 1031 exchange, there's another way you can save on your tax bill with capital gains. When you sell a property, any profit you make is taxable under capital gains, but the tax rate for long-term capital gains, which is usually more than one year, tends to be lower than the regular income tax rate.

It's important you understand and take advantage of these tax benefits once you start investing because they can really enhance your profitability. However, even if you know all of this, nothing replaces a qualified tax professional to oversee your business and point out any issues or more tax benefits that you can leverage. This professional can also ensure that you stay within the law—not that you'd ever be breaking it on purpose, but because it can accidentally happen if you don't fully understand what you're doing.

APPRECIATION

Let's now have a closer look at what property appreciation entails. This is one of the best ways for you to generate wealth with property investments. Because of that, it's vital that you understand exactly how it works and how you can take advantage of it, especially if you want to build long-term financial stability.

So, what exactly is appreciation? There are two types of appreciation – natural and forced. Natural appreciation is simply that—the natural tendency for prices to rise over time. While the price of everything goes up over time, you can also do your best to lean into natural appreciation by purchasing real estate in ideal locations. By choosing a property in a location that is or will soon be in an amazing neighborhood where there are good schools, a low crime rate, and great public transportation, the value of the property will tend to increase faster than others. But the market conditions, which are completely irrelevant to the property itself, are also an important factor. If the area of the property is prospering —that is, if the population, the economy, and job opportunities are growing—this will also influence the appreciation of the property.

Forced appreciation, on the other hand, is the concept of improving a property to increase its value. For example, taking a three-bedroom, one-and-a-half-bath and turning it into a four-bedroom, two-bath will immediately increase its value. This is incredibly powerful for the average investor because they can directly improve their investment and make more money rather than banking on external factors they can't control (like they would in, say, the stock market).

But why else does property appreciation matter so much for your real estate investments? Well, for one, it builds equity. This is because, as your properties appreciate, the discrepancy between the current market value and the amount you owe on your mortgage forms equity. You can use this equity by selling the property or remortgaging it. Either way, it provides you with the funds necessary for future investments. In other words, this appreciation can create leverage from your existing assets to acquire more properties. You can then use this higher equity in your properties as a down payment for new properties.

As time passes, property appreciation can significantly increase your net worth. This is huge! Do the work once, and watch your wealth grow over time.

CASH FLOW & GENERATING PASSIVE INCOME

In simple terms, cash flow is the amount of income left in your business after all the expenses like your mortgage, insurance, repairs, etc. have been paid. It is the lifeblood of any rental property business and vital for success.

Having a positive cash flow can also allow you to scale your business, meaning that for every property that you buy and rent out, this income increases—and due to inflation, it continues to increase while you pay the same mortgage (if you still have one). In turn, this means that your profit margins increase, as does your purchasing power. For example, if you have placed your money in a savings account, your purchasing power tends to decrease because, even though there's interest associated with the account, this interest is usually lower than the rate of inflation.

The amount of cash flow you can create largely depends on the property you have and the rental strategy you use. There are many different types of these strategies you can use, and you have to find the one that works best for you.

Short- and long-term are the most popular ones. Long-term leases happen when you rent out your property for more than six months, while short-term leases are usually for less time. While long-term rentals often involve renting the property to tenants, short-term rentals usually involve Airbnbing your property, especially if your property is in a location where there are plenty of tourist attractions. However, keep in mind that if you're going to rent out your property for short-term stays, doing so usually involves a lot more maintenance and upkeep than long-term leases. Even so, you can charge more, meaning your rental income is often higher.

Predicting the cash flow of a property can be difficult, but by using historical and industry data, you can get a realistic estimate of what it would be. We will get into the details of cash flow later in the book. However, if you can generate enough positive cash flow, you can reap the holy grail for most real estate investors: passive income.

Passive income is one of the most sought-after benefits of being a real estate investor and the central strategy of many. It refers to the income of money earned with almost no effort on your behalf, though it can provide you with financial security and freedom. I am telling you, there is almost nothing as satisfying as getting a check month after month while doing very little to no work.

As alluded to above, rental income is the main source of passive income in the real estate world. When you rent out a property, the rent paid by tenants comes every month. This is one of the most reliable sources of income in real estate because tenants have to pay rent if they want to live on the property. I cannot overstate how life changing it is the first time you get paid rent rather than paying it or a mortgage.

LEVERAGE

Leveraging debt to build wealth is a very attractive part of real estate investing and is a great tool that will allow you to increase your potential returns by using the money you borrow to acquire properties that produce more income. Let's have a closer look at it.

Leverage in the context of real estate investing is when you combine the capital you have and the funds that you borrow, usually in the form of a loan or a mortgage, to buy investment properties. The main goal here is to increase your returns. Leverage also means that you can utilize the power of other people's money (OPM) – most commonly, the bank's or that of private investors. This is done by securing financing from lenders where you use a small amount of your own money to do it, which in turn frees up more of your available capital to put into improving the property or for anything else that you want to invest in.

For example, let's say a property is priced at $300,000 and the bank is willing to lend me up to 80% off the asking price. In this case, the bank will lend me $240,000 in the form of a mortgage. This means that I only have to put $60,000 of my own money for a down payment. Basically, I am paying $60,000 to get a $300,000 asset that will appreciate and be worth more in the future!

If you're thinking you could never come up with $60,000 for a down payment, don't worry. This is just an example, and we'll be talking about ways to find and create little-to-no-money-down deals later in the book.

But the real benefit here is that you can significantly amplify your returns on your own investments. For easy math, let's say you have $100,000 in cash to invest (again, please don't worry if you don't – this is an example). You could simply use that money to purchase a property that would cost $100,000 right away. If in a year, that property appreciated by 5% , you would have $5,000 more. But if you leverage, instead of buying the property with all the money you have right away, you leverage that $100,000 and use it for a down payment on a property that costs $500,000. If within a year, that property appreciates the same 5% , you would have $25,000 more! That's $20,000 more by using the power of leverage!

There are some considerations you have to take into account when you're leveraging debt. While it's a great strategy to increase your wealth, it's not without risks. For instance, it's vital that you can cover the mortgage payments and other expenses related to the rental. You also can't forget about the interest on your borrowed money. Moreover, think about market volatility, as real estate markets can fluctuate, and in some cases, properties might not appreciate for some time. Leverage use can increase your returns, but they can also increase your risk. So, make sure that you have a diversified portfolio to help you mitigate some of that risk.

Leveraging debt is a wonderful long-term strategy to build wealth. As time passes, your properties appreciate, and with that, your rental income grows, so you can pay down the debt and accumulate significant wealth while your portfolio continues to produce income and stays diversified.

KEY TAKEAWAYS

- Real estate investing has created 90% of the world's millionaires—and you could be one of them.
- There are major tax benefits to real estate investing. Many successful investors pay less in taxes than most Americans, even though they typically make more income.
- Real estate has been a proven and reliable investment class, in large part due to appreciation: the natural or forced increase in value of the asset over time.
- Cash flow is king and the lifeblood of any business, including real estate.
- Leveraging debt is a powerful tool that allows you to buy expensive assets for a fraction of the cost.
- Tax benefits + appreciation + cash flow + leverage = the secret sauce to wealth building with real estate.

2

THE TOP 5 REAL ESTATE INVESTMENTS THAT CAN CHANGE YOUR LIFE

Ninety percent of all millionaires become so through owning real estate.

— ANDREW CARNEGIE

There are seemingly endless types of real estate investments, but five stand above the rest and have proven to be an approachable vehicle for ordinary people to become rich. Each category has its own pros and cons, so it will be your job, in line with your business plan, to choose the best option for your real estate investing journey.

One of the best parts of real estate investing is its flexibility. You can change your strategy along the way or employ many at once. It is, however, best to choose one strategy to get started with and stick to for a while before switching or adding more.

Let's dig deeper into each of these top five investment types to help you understand which may be more aligned with your goals as you begin your path in real estate.

RESIDENTIAL REAL ESTATE

Residential real estate is a simple entry point for any new investor. It's popular because it has a lower barrier to entry regarding both cost and knowledge. Even seasoned investors who go into other real estate industries sometimes include residential properties in their portfolios because they understand the value of diversification.

As you might expect, residential real estate refers to properties meant for people to live in. It has distinct advantages that we will discuss, along with the various types of properties within this category. These properties are everywhere, as everyone needs a place to live. They consist of single-family homes, townhouses, mobile homes, condominiums, apartment buildings, and multifamily properties, such as duplexes, triplexes, and quadplexes.

ADVANTAGES OF RESIDENTIAL PROPERTY

So, what are the benefits of owning residential property?

To start, these real estate assets have a continuous market demand level, making this category less volatile than others. However, it is essential to realize that variations are still possible. Residential properties are appealing because they have this particular characteristic of diversifying your real estate portfolio. You can buy any of them, including multifamily units, condominiums, and single-family houses.

Also, residential buildings have the benefit of providing consistent long-term rental revenue. Furthermore, they have higher appreciation rates than other real estate categories, allowing for the progressive expansion of your wealth over time.

As a real estate investor and an investor in general, you must often give up on different investments for various reasons. Residential properties are one of the simplest, most reliable, safest, and steadiest ways to build wealth. You can profit from these properties by renting, holding, fixing, and selling them. This type of property is also much easier to finance than the ones I'll discuss later in this section. This is because residential properties have significantly more financing choices than other types of assets.

DISADVANTAGES OF RESIDENTIAL PROPERTY

While residential properties might be more resistant to the changes in the market, they are also vulnerable to more significant economic cycles. Because of this, thorough research is required before making this sort of purchase.

On top of this, managing these properties can take a significant amount of time. If you don't have a property manager, you have to interact with and manage tenants yourself. You will face tenant-related concerns, such as background checks, resolving maintenance requests, rent payment issues, random appliances and equipment breaking, etc. There's also the property's upkeep, which must be done regularly to keep it in excellent condition and attract higher-quality renters.

There's also the dreaded vacancy issue. If someone isn't paying you rent to live in the property, you still have to pay the mortgage on time and out of pocket, and your cash flow decreases. So, it's essential to account for an appropriate vacancy rate in your financial analysis for when these things happen before you even buy the deal.

Finally, the landlord-tenant laws, which may be complicated at times, apply to residential premises. Regulations can differ by location, so it's crucial to know the rules you must follow, especially regarding evictions, squatters' rights, etc.

While these disadvantages may seem scary, don't let them stop you. There are many ways to mitigate the risk of these situations, plan for them, and strategize ways to handle them, which we will go through later in this book.

COMMERCIAL REAL ESTATE

Commercial real estate is considered a step above regarding the complexity and cost of investment. Commercial properties cater to businesses. When it comes to tenants, while leases might take a little longer to be drawn, you can expect tenants to stay there longer, which allows you better cash flow.

When it comes to commercial real estate, there's a lot more diversity. You have office buildings, industrial facilities, or warehouses, for example. Nonetheless, the cost to invest in these properties is higher than the amounts you might be used to seeing in residential properties. Let's look at the various types of commercial real estate.

Office buildings are among the most common and are self-explanatory. They can serve as workspaces for single or many tenants and range in size from small offices to towering skyscrapers. These spaces can be filled by anyone, from a lawyer's office to a mortgage company, marketing firm, etc.

Retail properties include malls, shopping centers, freestanding stores, and restaurants, another common commercial real estate category. They are all structured to cater to businesses that directly service consumers, including clothing stores, grocery stores, daycares, and so on.

Warehouses or industrial buildings, such as manufacturing facilities, distribution centers, and others, are other commercial options. These are typically integrated into logistic hubs to facilitate the movement or creation of products.

Hotels and other hospitality properties are also classified as commercial real estate. They include, as previously mentioned, hotels, motels, bed & breakfasts, resorts, or any other sort of lodging facility.

Then we have multifamily apartment complexes, which, while residential, can also be considered commercial real estate if they have five or more units.

Lastly, there are commercial buildings known as special-purpose properties, which are created for highly unique uses. They vary from educational institutions to healthcare facilities and even religious institutions.

ADVANTAGES OF COMMERCIAL REAL ESTATE

There are plenty of benefits when it comes to investing in commercial real estate, but here are the six major ones:

1. There's a much higher income potential because commercial properties often charge higher rents than residential properties.
2. Commercial properties with an excellent location might also appreciate more than residential properties.
3. There is potential for much higher-quality tenants with solid finances, which reduces the risk of tenants not paying rent or damaging the property.
4. Commercial tenants tend to have much longer leases, which allows you to have a much more stable rental income.
5. These properties can have triple net leases where tenants take care of bills like maintenance, insurance, and property taxes. However, for this to happen, you typically charge tenants a lower rent.
6. Suppose you have specialized assets or the ability to build to suit. In that case, you can attract tenants that, in turn, sign leases with higher rents and stay far longer than traditional commercial tenants. For example, let's say the USDA is looking for office space. They want to rent out your property, but need the space renovated to meet specific requirements from the government. If you can meet their specifications, the USDA will likely pay you a high-rent, sign-a-10+-year lease, and renew this long lease.

DISADVANTAGES OF COMMERCIAL REAL ESTATE

Despite all these advantages, commercial properties have certain downsides that must be carefully considered. One such disadvantage is the significantly higher initial expenditure necessary to invest in these properties. Purchasing a commercial property is frequently more expensive than buying a residential home, so a thorough understanding of deal analysis, financing, market trends, and a pulse on the local business ecosystem is essential to making effective investment decisions.

Also, keep in mind that the agreements for commercial leases tend to be more complex than those for residential properties. It's always best to bring in an attorney specializing in commercial leases. The same goes for the upkeep of your commercial property, which often requires more specialized professionals to work on it.

RAW LAND INVESTMENTS

Depending on what you do with it, raw land investments can range from very simple to being the most complex type of real estate investment out there. The two simple ways of making money with land investments are to buy and hold the property or rent it out as is. The buy-and-hold strategy is when an investor purchases a plot of land, keeps it for years, and sells it for a much higher price years or decades later. The other simple way to capitalize on raw land is to rent it out. This can be as simple as renting your land to farmers to grow their crops or as complex as renting to large companies like McDonald's, for instance, that want to build a location on your land. In situations like this, the company usually rents the land, but pays to erect a building themselves.

So, when do raw land investments get complicated? One word: developments. Many investors love this strategy, which is when investors take raw land and turn it into residential or commercial property by building on it. This commitment, however, adds a layer of intricacy and understanding that demands prior experience, and I'll emphasize that raw land may only be profitable if you have the necessary expertise. If you turn this land into a residential or commercial property, you will face a lengthy building period, significant upfront financial obligations, and the need to wait for eventual sales or tenant occupancy. In addition, a large amount of bureaucratic red tape and effort is required.

Still, investors love this strategy because they have almost total control over it—they can build anything they want the way they want it. However, there are things you have to consider, such as location, that will help you choose what you should build. Also, depending on the area, you can build any property, from residential to commercial or even more specialized properties, if you get it appropriately zoned.

Although there's more risk in this strategy of developing raw land, investors love to seize on these opportunities because when done correctly, they can make a killing off these deals.

ADVANTAGES OF RAW LAND INVESTMENTS

An obvious advantage of these investments is your creative control over what you do with them—the possibilities are almost endless! You can build the property you have envisioned. If it's well located, it can have great potential for appreciation, just like residential or commercial properties.

A lesser-known benefit to land investments is that you will pay little to no property taxes on your undeveloped land until a property is built, so your holding costs are much cheaper than purchasing an existing property.

And finally, when executed correctly, investors can make significant money from developing residential or commercial properties on land they purchase.

DISADVANTAGES OF RAW LAND INVESTMENTS

Like anything else, these investments also come with disadvantages and risks, as you might imagine. For instance, local zoning laws and regulations can significantly impact what you can do with the land. They can stop you from building a commercial or residential property altogether, for instance. Before buying raw land, you should inform yourself and do thorough research on what you can and can't build.

Also, when it's time to build a property, the costs can be steep. This process is called developing the land, and you don't only have to buy materials and personnel to build it; you also need to pay for a myriad of things before you can build anything there. For instance, you may need to purchase utility installation, grading, environmental assessments, permitting fees, or road construction.

You also have to consider the current market conditions when you expect to buy raw land because this timing can affect its value. Another thing that you need to consider is access to infrastructure such as electricity, water, or sewers, which might increase the price even more if you have to install all of that.

REIT INVESTING

REIT investing, which stands for real estate investment trust investing, is a great way to enter the real estate industry. A REIT is a company solely aiming to manage, own, or finance real estate properties to generate income. In other words, you can look at REIT as a stock investment because stock is traded there, similar to a mutual fund dedicated to real estate. This way, you can buy shares of properties without purchasing, managing, financing, or paying a down payment on them.

Because they are like stocks, REITs are far more liquid than actually investing in a property. You can simply sell the shares and get money in your account, which doesn't happen as fast when you sell a property (this usually demands a lengthy process). REIT investments can apply to any property, from residential to commercial and anything in between.

While most REITs specialize in real estate investment, there are a few specialized REITs that hold specific types of properties if you want to diversify your portfolio. That being said, let's quickly go over the main types of REITs you can find.

There's a market for REITs: companies that lend money to real estate owners through mortgages or loans, whose earnings mainly come from net interest margins. Equity REITs, on the other hand, are more common. These companies often own and manage income-producing properties, so their income comes from rent, which often comes in monthly dividends as if you were receiving rent when you own a property. Then, there are hybrid REITs, a mix of the two above.

While these are the main types of REITs, they can also be divided into subgroups, such as publicly traded REITs, which you often find in the stock market; public non-traded REITs, which don't trade in exchanges but are still registered with the SEC; and private REITs, which only institutional investors have access to.

If you're starting out, publicly traded REITs are the easiest to start investing in. You can simply do this by having a brokerage account and purchasing shares of the REIT. Unlike individual company stocks, REITs tend not to grow in value as much, but pay dividends instead.

ADVANTAGES OF REITS

I've mentioned some advantages of REITs, such as being highly liquid, but there's more. Investing in REITs can expand your portfolio's diversification, even if you're just a real estate investor. You can invest in different properties you wouldn't otherwise invest in.

Furthermore, cash flow is stable because you receive dividends, and you don't have to worry about screening tenants, so you know you will receive money from the REIT regardless. Lastly, REITs are flexible when it comes to adjusting your risk.

DISADVANTAGES OF REITS

As I've pointed out, don't expect a lot of growth from REITs, mainly because that's not really their way of operating, as any surplus they get is distributed in the form of dividends.

Also, the dividends you receive are taxed as regular income and are often associated with high transaction fees, though this depends on the REIT you buy shares from.

TAX LIENS

Tax lien investing is often overlooked by real estate investors. What is a tax lien anyway?

Essentially, a tax lien is a legal claim against a business or individual's assets when they fail to pay taxes to the government. If the obligation to pay is not fulfilled, the creditor can repossess the assets. However, as a private investor, these claims can be traded and exchanged, and you can generate profit from those transactions. Of course, as with any investment, there are risks, and you must understand the rules.

In simpler terms, if a homeowner fails to pay their property taxes, the local government can place a lien on the property, which, as we've seen, is a legal claim. The home can only be refinanced or sold once the debt is paid. When there's a lien, a tax lien certificate is issued, which shows the amount of debt plus any interest added. These certificates can then be auctioned off to investors. When investors acquire the certificate, they must pay back the total amount immediately. Then, the homeowner must pay the investor all the money they invested plus interest, often between 10% and 25%.

Keep in mind that there's usually a repayment schedule between six months and three years. The legal claim comes in if the homeowner fails to repay their lien. If this happens, the owner of the tax lien—in this case, the real estate investor—has a legal claim to the property, and it is now theirs to do with what they wish. The investor can then get paid with either a 10% -25% interest payment or an entirely new property to keep, sell, or rent out. This can be a huge investment opportunity!

ADVANTAGES OF TAX LIEN INVESTING

Tax liens can see a higher rate of return than the stock market, anywhere between 10% -25% . They are secure investments, as they are in first position—meaning, they get first priority to be paid out. They are also more affordable to get started in, and they don't require as much of a learning curve as other types of investing.

Once you lock in a certain interest rate for your lien, that is what you get. Another big advantage to these investments is they are paid out by the government rather than by individuals or companies, so they're enforced by law and not as subject to fraud.

DISADVANTAGES OF TAX LIEN INVESTING

You have no control when the taxes are paid, which means you may have to wait a long time to get paid yourself. Another risk is that the rules and regulations vary county by county, so some might sell liens for properties with little to no value. As a result, you really have to do your due diligence with the county you are buying from.

Lastly, there's not a ton of information available on tax lien investing or resources to learn about this topic. Most people don't know much about it because tax lien investors prefer to stick to themselves to keep the competition out.

KEY TAKEAWAYS

- Residential real estate is the most common and often easiest way to get started in real estate investing.
- Commercial real estate costs more to invest in than residential real estate, but often has higher rents, longer leases, and higher-quality tenants.
- Raw land investments that are development deals are complicated, high-risk, and high-reward deals that can pay off exponentially with the right approach. These investments are not beginner friendly.

- REITs are the easiest way to invest in real estate, as no property management is involved.
- Tax liens are one of the best-kept secrets in real estate investing. They allow you to pay someone's unpaid taxes for them and get paid back before even the banks and the government—or you—get to keep the property.

Regardless of which of these five types of investments you choose, due diligence is absolutely essential. It's the only way you can mitigate any financial losses, and the only way you can make the right decisions.

In the following chapter, we will go through various investing strategies in depth. I will focus on the most common ones and give you advice on how you can choose the one that suits you best.

3

THE SWISS ARMY KNIFE OF REAL ESTATE INVESTING & THE BEST INVESTMENT STRATEGIES

Real estate is an imperishable asset, ever increasing in value. It is the most solid security that human ingenuity has devised. It is the basis of all security and about the only indestructible security.

— RUSSELL SAGE

A Swiss Army knife is the world's gold standard of pocketknives, known for its reliability, versatility, and durability. This iconic tool is essentially the right tool for any job. It can help solve just about any problem, and can even save those in an emergency.

So, what is the Swiss Army knife of real estate investing? Your brain. It's all the knowledge you have about real estate investing.

You may be thinking that you don't know much yet about this topic, so you don't have much of a Swiss Army knife. However, the best part is that anyone can develop and learn about the ins and outs of real estate investing for little to no money invested. You don't have to have an expensive degree, a fancy job, or a network of exclusive people. The education needed for real estate investing is accessible through the Internet, books, conferences, networking, organizations, etc. You can learn about the different investing strategies to employ, the intricacies of a specific property type, the multitude of ways to finance a deal, the details of the local laws and ordinances in your area, the little-known ways to use the tax code to your advantage—you name it, you can learn it! The sky is the limit, and the more you learn, the more tools you will have at your disposal to solve just about any problem that comes your way. At the end of the day, that's what real estate investors are— problem solvers.

One of the best tools you can have as an investor is a thorough knowledge of the varied investment strategies. Knowing about all of them will allow you to be as flexible as possible when issues arise or when you need to pivot. They can help you see big money-making opportunities that other people can't.

So, let's get into the most popular investment strategies.

THE FIX-AND-FLIP

The Fix-and-Flip is perhaps the most popular strategy investors start with outside of rental property investing. With this strategy, investors purchase a property below market value, renovate it to increase its value, and sell it at market value.

These properties are typically distressed or need much fixing to make them attractive. So, an investor needs to have a vision of what the end project will look like, how much it will cost to complete the project, and how much they can sell the property for to cover their purchase and renovation costs and to make a profit. Many people are afraid to invest in ugly-looking properties or ones with more significant issues beyond cosmetic ones. However, when executed correctly, this strategy can be highly profitable.

So why doesn't the owner do it themselves to make money off their property? Typically, the owners of these properties are not investors, so they don't know how, or even that they can. Even if they did, they may not have the money, time, or desire to renovate it themselves. This is good for investors because, most of the time, these owners want to get rid of their property as fast as possible, so they are willing to sell quicker and at a much lower price.

However, fix-and-flip is easier said than done. Significant research is needed when dealing with distressed properties. Doing an in-depth financial analysis and careful due diligence is required before purchasing these properties to ensure you accurately budget your finances and time to avoid losing money on the deal. It's vital to account for all that could go wrong or not according to plan because, by nature of the business, it will. On the flip side, if these properties do not require considerable changes and you can't increase their value enough, you'll get little or no profit from the sale.

Foreclosures are the most common type of distressed property. These occur when property owners default on their mortgages, causing the bank or another financial organization that granted the loan to repossess the property. Because of this, such properties are often more affordable. In other cases, foreclosure homes might not require renovations. This is great for investors because they can sell them at a higher price without incurring remodeling costs. Imagine how great that would be!

There are also short sales, which happen when the owner sells the property at a lower price than that of the comparable properties in a given market. This can happen because of numerous circum-stances, but the most common is simply because the seller wants to complete the sale as soon as possible. Nonetheless, it presents an excellent opportunity for those looking to buy. Another instance of when this might occur is through auctions, where you can find properties to buy at a lower price.

With the fix-and-flip strategy (and the real estate business in general), networking is essential. This is because having connec-tions with developers or real estate agents allows the opportunity to get off-market deals, meaning these properties have yet to be put on the market for everyone to see. As a result, you can nego-tiate a lower price for them.

IMPROVEMENTS AND RENOVATIONS

While sometimes you don't need to renovate the property that much to increase its value, most of the time, you do. And there are many different things you might need or want to do to accomplish that.

The best improvements that can increase a property's value are simple cosmetic upgrades such as a fresh coat of paint on the outside wall, interior renovations such as flooring, or exterior changes such as landscaping. These are great because they often make a big difference at a small cost to the investor. Then, there are structural repairs that are usually more expensive and essential. For instance, there may be roof and foundation repairs or any other structural issues vital to the property.

Some improvements fall in between cosmetic upgrades and structural repairs. Remodeling the kitchen or bathroom or adding a room or useable square footage is a substantial improvement that could significantly boost a property's value. This increases the property's worth and makes it more attractive, so more people may be interested in buying it, thus increasing its demand as well.

Other things that can increase property value include improving energy efficiency or updating essential systems such as HVAC and electrical installations. Keep in mind that it is critical to ensure that any upgrade or renovation complies with local building rules and that the necessary licenses are secured.

WHAT TO CONSIDER FINANCIALLY

To execute a fix-and-flip properly and successfully, you must take into account a few financial considerations. Keep in mind the following things while creating your financial plan.

First, you must factor in the property's purchasing cost. You should buy the property for a price lower than its current market value. The lower the buying price, the greater the potential upside, and the more wiggle room you have for mistakes. You also have to think about the renovation budget. The goal here is to guarantee that you can still make a significant profit when the home sells after deducting both the purchase and remodeling costs. Minimizing delays or cost overruns during renovation will be critical to your success.

If you can get enough financing for the purchase and renovation, it can help you immensely in the event unexpected costs and delays arise. These things happen all the time. Again, the purchasing cost and renovations have to be lower than what you sell the property for to profit from the investment.

To know the price you should sell the renovated property for, you must research the local market and check comps (comparable properties in the area). For example, if you buy a one-bedroom and plan to make it a two-bedroom, research how much two-bedrooms in the same area are going for.

CHALLENGES AND RISKS OF THE FIX-AND-FLIP STRATEGY

Of course, there are challenges and risks to every investment strategy. Market fluctuations always happen, so they are a risk, regardless of your plan. This is mainly due to the normal movements of the economy, which can be up or down at any given moment. Even specific local market conditions can affect the price of properties.

However, there are three main challenges when undertaking a fix-and-flip. Let's take a closer look at them.

ESTIMATING THE SCOPE OF THE PROJECT

Properly assessing what is needed to improve a property is imperative to a successful fix-and-flip. This information forms the baseline for everything else. If you can figure out precisely what needs to be done and who will be doing it, you can plan much more accurately for your budget and timeline while lowering the risk of not making your target profit.

Besides knowing what needs to be done to the actual property, you also need to learn about any external factors like zoning requirements, permits, ordinances, or tax laws. You also need to determine if you want to put some sweat equity in the deal and personally paint rooms and tear down walls, or if you want to hire contractors or companies to do a partial or complete renovation.

If you have the skills and time to do a lot of the renovation yourself, your profit margin will be much higher. Some investors love doing renovations themselves, while others don't. Not everyone has the skills or time to do it themselves, so they have to hire everything out.

ESTIMATING COSTS

Estimating costs for a renovation can be tricky. If you set a budget to use for your renovations, but in reality it costs more than what you budgeted, this could mean that your profit margins will shrink.

Trying to guess how much money you need without making sound calculations can be quite expensive in the real estate industry. This is why accurately estimating the project's scope and planning it ahead of time is so important. First, having an accurate understanding of what needs to be done to the property lowers the chances of an expensive surprise that will eat up all your profits or, worse, put you in debt. Second, you'll have a much more accurate picture of the total renovation cost. So, it is vital to decide beforehand if and what you will do yourself and what parts you are hiring out.

There are a lot of questions that need to be answered before you get into a deal like this. Do you need a plumber, roofer, electrician, or carpenter? How much do they typically charge for what you need to be done, and how long will it take? How do these things impact your bottom line and overall strategy?

To reiterate, if you have the skills and time to do a lot of the renovation yourself, your profit margin will be much higher. However, don't think you have to do this to make a lot of money. Many investors hire everything out and still make a lot of money at the end of a fix-and-flip. It's all about accurately planning and executing the project.

When planning the finances for your project, you'll have to consider more than just the renovation. Acquiring the property is the first cost, and usually the most expensive. And while you might come across low or no-money-down financing claims, these can often be false. So, when you do come across such claims, there are a few things that you should consider. For instance, while the interest on borrowed money can be deducted from your tax return, it's not 100% deductible. This means that every penny you spend on interest adds to the amount you will have to earn on the sale. Also, if you get a mortgage or even a HELOC (home equity line of credit) to finance your investment, remember that only the interest is deductible. Everything else – like taxes, insurance, or principal – is not.

When beginning with a fix-and-flip strategy, there are ways to limit your financial risk and maximize your potential return. In other words, avoid overpaying for the property and ensure you know how much the necessary renovations will be before investing in that property. Here, you can use the 70% rule, which dictates that you shouldn't pay more than 70% of the property's after-repair value (ARV) minus any necessary repairs. The ARV is what the property is worth after the renovations are done. Here's an example:

Let's say the property's ARV is $200,000 and the repairs are $30,000. You shouldn't pay more than $110,000, as $200,000 x 0.70 = $140,000 minus $30,000 = $110,000.

Of course, sometimes you have to pay a little more for renovations because of unforeseen circumstances, but calculating the AVR is a good way to narrow down how much you should pay for a property. While correctly estimating a fix-and-flip budget can be difficult, it's not impossible.

ESTIMATING TIME

Nailing down an accurate timeline for fix-and-flips is just as challenging. Not having enough time budgeted is one of the biggest mistakes new real estate investors make with this strategy. While this method is relatively faster than buy-and-hold to make profits, it's still time-consuming and often takes more time to see it through. Once you are the property owner, you have to either do or oversee the renovations, which can take a lot of time.

Going through the average processes means demolition (which is common) and construction. Once the renovations are done, you still need to inspect the property and ensure everything is in order; otherwise, you will have to spend more time and money fixing it. Also, unexpected delays happen during renovations all the time. Whether a particular contractor is behind deadline, the delivery of parts is delayed, or there's a required specific local permit that you were unaware of, issues tend to pop up when you least expect them. Lastly, there's the selling of the property, which can also take more time than investors think.

While many of these challenges seem frustrating and scary to a new investor, they are par for the course. The important thing is allocating enough cushion time for the project without losing money. While these issues of estimating the scope of the project, costs, and time are common, if you do proper due diligence, thoroughly assess the conditions of the property and what it will take to complete the project, add in enough cushion for costs and time, you can mitigate a lot of the risks. Fix-and-flips can be highly profitable and, dare I say, fun if you're willing to put in the effort necessary.

The element that makes this strategy different from most of the others is this aspect of project management. You not only need to understand the real estate market, but you also have to be an expert when it comes to juggling deadlines, contracts, schedules, people, and many other moving parts. There may be a learning curve, but you'll get better and better over time and be able to manage many renovations at once, making you a large amount of wealth.

BUY-AND-HOLD STRATEGY

The buy-and-hold strategy is the most popular for real estate investors. As the name indicates, it involves buying and holding on to a property for a certain period (usually at least a year or more) before selling it. However, while you hold it, you get rental income by renting the property to tenants. This is perhaps one of the most profitable investment strategies because while you're getting rental income for years, the property is appreciating, so when you sell it, you are likely to sell it for more than you've paid. In theory, the longer you hold the property, the more you earn.

You can do this with almost any property type, from a duplex to a warehouse to a commercial property. Regardless of the property type you invest in, securing financing is typically key to maximizing your profits. The idea here is to invest a smaller amount upfront for a down payment to get a loan paid for by the rent your tenants pay you.

So, for example, let's say you put 20% down ($60,000) for a $300,000 property. You will have a loan of $240,000—with interest, of course—that other people are paying down for you! So, essentially, you're paying $60,000 for a property that will likely appreciate being much higher than a $300,000 value, making you hundreds of thousands of dollars in the future. On top of this, if you play your cards right, money will go into your pocket every month until then from the cash flow of your property.

Another important aspect here is that, as you pay your mortgage from the rent your tenants pay you, you are acquiring equity, which is to say that every time you pay your mortgage, you are acquiring a little bit more of the property, thereby increasing your wealth. Plus, the equity you build can be used for any future investments you want to make; this is called leverage. There are also the tax benefits I've previously mentioned, such as tax credits, depreciation deductions, or capital gains tax benefits from buy-and-hold rental properties.

Do you see the magic of real estate investing yet?!

The very first step when considering a buy-and-hold strategy is to look for and compare properties. Of all the steps, this one might be the most tedious, but it's important. Having a realtor by your side can make this process a lot faster because they can narrow down properties of potential interest and even help you through online auctions or through their multiple listing service (MLS), which is a database that realtors have access to. Then, you either purchase the property right away or finance it, which is similar to the process of buying a home.

Once all of that is done, you will have to rent out the property and manage it, which can be time-consuming in the beginning. But once you've rented it out, depending on the quality of your property, it doesn't have to be this way going forward. To find tenants, you need to market the property well to attract the best ones, screen the potential tenants by running background checks to ensure they can afford the rent, create a lease agreement, understand all the local and state laws, and get your landlord insurance.

Another popular strategy for buy-and-hold investors is short-term or mid-term rentals. This is when an investor buys a property, furnishes it, pays all utilities, and rents it out typically anywhere between one night to one month for a short-term vacation rental or anywhere from 3-9 months for a mid-term rental. Vacation rentals are typically high-maintenance properties because they need to be constantly flipped, cleaned, supplied, and guests can be demanding. However, in the right area, these properties can make investors high returns, oftentimes high enough to pay property managers to take care of all of the guest headaches that inevitably pop up.

Mid-term or medium-term rentals are usually for traveling professionals who work on a multi-month contract and need a place to stay. They are often a sweet spot for investors because these tenants are typically high-quality, with good records and reliable income to pay the rent. The best part is sometimes their company gives out high stipends or pays rent for them. Overall, these professionals are much more similar to having tenants than having guests in a short-term rental. They tend to be lower-maintenance and treat the property more like their own apartment than a vacation rental.

Buy-and-hold properties usually come with a lot of maintenance. Some items are best to take care of right away when you buy a property, while others you may be able to wait on fixing if you need to save up for them. This is why it's so important to pay attention to the ages of things like HVAC, roofing, appliances, etc., when doing due diligence of the property and financial analysis. When it comes to maintenance of the property, you have to consider updating carbon monoxide and smoke alarms, keeping up with the maintenance of the HVAC system and any other system, as well as managing structural issues that come up during an inspection, such as foundation issues. It's particularly important that you check for any structural issues before renting the property out so you can fix them right away and avoid a more expensive problem down the line.

Other tasks entailed in managing rental properties include rent collection and security deposits, keeping track of taxes, handling maintenance requests, getting proper insurance, dealing with utilities, and paying mortgages.

RISKS AND CHALLENGES OF THE BUY-AND-HOLD STRATEGY

The biggest challenge in managing rental properties is tenant management, which largely involves dealing with tenant issues as well as vacancies. The maintenance of the property is another challenge, requiring you to regularly maintain the property, do repairs, and pay for unexpected costs.

With a buy-and-hold, you also need to think about an exit strategy, but unlike the fix-and-flip, this exit strategy is long-term. The most common exit strategies with the buy-and-hold are selling the property, using it as a retirement home, or simply passing it on to your children.

While you are renting the property, you should keep an eye on the housing market trends so you can understand the current and potential future of the housing market and know what your next step should be. Having a good grasp on the market will allow you to make the best decision when it comes to continuing to rent the property and know when it is a good time to sell for maximum profit.

This brings us to the next step: knowing when to sell your property. One way to find out if it's a good time to sell is if comparable properties begin to depreciate (and you already want to sell the property, of course). Another big reason to sell is if your current investment no longer serves your needs and financial goals. You should be regularly evaluating if your investments still align with your strategy and ultimate goals. Other reasons investors sell is that the property is costing them more money, time, or effort than anticipated. If the property is going downhill, it's better for them to cut their losses than hire a property manager to do their work for them.

If you do decide to sell, it's important that you consider taxes beforehand. When you sell a property, you have to pay capital gain taxes, and the time you sell your property will dictate how much tax you pay. For instance, if you've owned the property for less than a year, you will pay short-term capital gains, but if you've held on to the property for longer than that, you'll get preferential tax rates because of long-term capital gains.

WHOLESALING

Wholesaling is a real estate strategy that is quite different from the others we've seen here so far. With wholesaling, you are essentially the middle point between sellers and buyers when it comes to making a transaction. So, you don't have to purchase the property yourself (well, kind of). Instead, you earn money by getting a commission when the sale is done.

While wholesale carries a much lower risk and you can make money faster, the profits are substantially lower than with other strategies. However, it's a great way to get into the real estate market if you don't have a lot of money to invest in properties.

The very first step with wholesaling is to find a distressed property, but unlike the fix-and-flip strategy, you're not purchasing the property. Instead, you negotiate with the seller to secure a purchase contract at a price that is much lower than the market value (it has to be much lower for this strategy to work). This is so that when you sell the property without any renovations done, you can sell for a profit that is likely still below market, but higher than the price you've paid.

After you've conducted your research and found a distressed property, you need to do your due diligence and your math. Here, finding out the property's fair market value will give you a little more information about how much profit you can make. You also have to look at comparable properties, cash-on-cash returns, and occupancy rates, as well as determine the cost of repairs. With this information, you can calculate the ARV. Then, you can calculate the maximum offer, which tells you how much higher you can go pricewise while still making a profit on the investment.

If all your math and due diligence check out, you need to contact the seller and tell them about your role as a wholesaler and how your services might be a great way to help them sell the property. You have to clearly explain how the role of a wholesaler can help them because many people might not be familiar with this strategy. Then, you have to obtain a property contract, but before that, you need to present your offer. Keep in mind that the property contract should have included the right to assign the contract to a different person (that's the main role of a wholesaler) and include some contingencies, especially one that states that you can back off from a deal if you can't find a buyer before the expiration of the contract.

Once that is done, you have to find a cash buyer, and here, your networking will really come in handy, as you can contact investors who might be interested in a fix-and-flip strategy. Alternatively, you can also contact real estate agencies and ask for a list of cash purchases made recently in the area.

When you do find a buyer, you have to reassign the contract to the buyer and make sure you get paid for the work you've done.

The most important aspect of being able to pull off this strategy is having the right connections. As a wholesaler, your most important job is to create a network of buyers and sellers, such as flippers (those who do fix-and-flip strategies), landlords (who want to sell), real estate agents, and other professionals in the industry. So, when you sign the purchase contract, you don't necessarily close the property, but when you sell it, the buyer assumes the rights and obligations of the contract. When you do this, you obtain what is called in the industry a "wholesale fee," which is usually around 5% of the property's value.

Some benefits of the wholesale strategy are, as I've mentioned, quick profits and low financial risk. Starting with wholesaling is also a great way to learn the ins and outs of real estate without investing too much money, as well as improve your negotiation skills. Also, you don't need to go through certain requirements that are needed with other strategies, such as checks on your credit score, and you don't need previous experience in how to renovate a property.

RISKS AND CONSIDERATIONS OF THE WHOLESALE STRATEGY

While the wholesale strategy is effectively lower on risk compared to other strategies, that doesn't necessarily mean it's risk free. Here, it's crucial that you have a great understanding of the local market to ensure that you get the purchase contract at a low price and manage to sell it for a profit. You also have to pay attention to legal and ethical compliance, such as local real estate laws and local regulations. If you fail to comply with them, your deal can fall through. Also, if you don't have a strong network of professionals and strong negotiation skills, your chances of being successful with this strategy are drastically reduced.

It's just as important to have a great marketing campaign and marketing team to look for potential buyers. This is because you need to be able to find a buyer fast, and the longer it takes to do this, the more money you lose. If it happens that you can't find a buyer, you need to have an exit strategy ready, which could potentially mean renegotiating the contract with the seller or simply walking away from the contract.

As you can see, the wholesale strategy is very different from other strategies we've seen so far. You need very different skills to make this strategy successful and find the best opportunities for you. However, if you are successful with it, you can make a great profit with much less upfront money.

If you want to make a profit with this strategy, you need to have great networking skills. This might be a little challenging if you haven't done so already, but it's something that you can work on.

You will not make any money with wholesaling until you have found suitable properties and investors. This means that there will be times when you've worked quite a bit on a property, but were unable to find a suitable investor in time, and so you've not only lost time but also your earnest money. You also have to consider the fact that distressed properties can be unpredictable because of how dependent they are on the other properties available.

HOUSE HACKING

House hacking is a strategy that is quite time-consuming. It involves the benefits of income generation through ownership. With this strategy, you usually purchase a multifamily property with multiple units where you will live in one and rent out the other units to tenants. A very important benefit to point out here is that you can almost offset your property expenses with the rent you generate while you build equity with the multifamily property. If you're just starting out, house hacking is a great strategy because you might be able to get a great loan, buy your first property, and generate income while doing it.

As I've mentioned before, if you're looking to buy your first property, conventional or traditional loans are the easiest and cheapest way to secure financing. But to make your strategy even easier to execute, if you have friends who are looking for a place to rent, you can have them occupy the other units. This way, you don't have to screen people that you don't know, and it's a much easier process this way.

Either way, if you follow through with this strategy, you will become an owner-occupant, which simply means that you will be living with your tenants on the same property. You still need to do some management, especially if you have to screen tenants and market the property. Nonetheless, this strategy has great benefits, from lowering your housing expenses to high cash flows, equity accumulation, and tax benefits linked to your property ownership. Let's look at an example.

You've bought a duplex for $300,000 with a 20% downpayment (or $60,000) and the remaining balance of the loan ($240,000) will be paid in the form of a fixed mortgage over 30 years with a 4% interest rate. This means that you will be paying $1,145.80 a month. Now, if you live in one unit of the house and rent out the other unit for $2,000 a month, the tenants will be paying more than you have to pay for your mortgage, plus you get $854.20 in profit that you can use to pay for repairs, taxes, or insurance. After only a few years, you would have built quite a bit of equity in the property while the property itself appreciated.

While you can use house hacking for many properties, some types work better than others. A multifamily home, for instance, is a great one, such as duplexes or triplexes. Alternatively, if you have an extra room that you won't be using, you can rent it out for the short term, such as using it as an Airbnb. This way, you don't have to always live with a tenant on your property, and you make more money on rent because short-term rentals usually yield a higher income.

RISKS AND CHALLENGES OF THE HOUSE HACKING STRATEGY

The biggest challenge when it comes to house hacking is managing the property. As discussed, you might be able to mitigate this challenge if you already know the tenants you're bringing in. If you don't, managing the property can be quite a time-consuming activity.

Also, you have to keep in mind that the level of privacy you experience is not the same as if you were living in a single unit.

Furthermore, remember to think of an exit strategy. Usually, this means moving out and renting out all the units once you are done paying the mortgage.

As you can see, this type of strategy is very different from the fix-and-flip or the buy-and-hold, but it might be ideal for you if you're looking for a primary property to live in. Still, it requires some effort and can be quite time-consuming, so keep those things in mind.

CHOOSING THE RIGHT STRATEGY FOR YOUR GOALS

As you can see, each investment method has its own distinct qualities and its own set of benefits and downsides. It is your responsibility to choose which technique best fits your present level as an investor. Recognize that extensive research is required when choosing a strategy at any given moment, as your selection will significantly influence your financial objectives, risk tolerance, and eventual success. Your strategy choice will also have a significant impact on your property acquisition method and, ultimately, the return on your investment.

How can one properly go through this assessment process? You've probably figured out what you want to do with your money at this time. If not, it is crucial to begin this process by outlining your financial goals. Ask yourself, "Am I aiming for short-term or long-term wealth or a combination of both?" Numerous key things must be examined to determine your answer. Consider cash flow, for instance, if you expect a consistent income stream from rental profits to fund costs. Also, ask yourself if you want to rely on property appreciation to increase your net worth, examine your risk tolerance, and determine your level of comfort with financial obligations.

The next stage is analyzing your resources, and here, you have to find out how much you have before picking a strategy. This is not only about your financial resources, but also your understanding of the strategies and the real estate industry as a whole. However, knowing the state of your finances will help you narrow down the types of strategies you can go for because some strategies need more upfront capital than others.

Time is another resource you need to take into account, as some of these strategies, such as buy-and-hold to then rent, will likely make you a landlord, which is significantly time-consuming. Of course, you can always hire a property management firm, but if you're starting out, that measure will take a lot of your profit. Lastly, having the necessary knowledge to pursue the strategy you want to perform is a must.

While choosing the investment strategy to use, you also have to take into account the current market conditions. Depending on how the market is going, different strategies might work better than others. But here, you should consider factors like the demand for rental properties or the current economic stability. Of course, location will also inform the strategy you might want to use, as well as the laws and regulations in that area.

There are factors that you have to dig into a little more in order to fully understand the right strategy for you to use. A risk-and-return analysis can really help you out by making a risk-reward profile for the different strategies you're considering, as well as helping you determine whether each strategy aligns with your goals. So, looking at financing risks, market volatility, and potential tenant problems might help you figure out the strategy for you. At the same time, you need to get an estimate of the returns you will have, which means you have to account for overall profitability and appreciation.

You must also take into consideration the diversification of your portfolio, and understand that adding different strategies will allow you to mitigate some of the risks and stabilize your portfolio. Keep in mind that some strategies complement one another so you can consolidate the diversification of your portfolio. However, being flexible and open to new strategies, as well as adjusting things as you see fit, will give you a leg up when mitigating risks. In other words, having a static strategy will not get you very far; you have to keep tweaking your strategies because the market is always evolving. The same is true for an exit strategy, which you have to set up for every single investment you make.

Once you figure out what strategies to use, you can start to narrow them down even further to land on one that is the most suitable for you at this point in your career. As I've said before, many young real estate investors prefer to start with the buy-and-hold strategy because it doesn't require much experience or initial capital. Here, you purchase a property, rent it out, and after a few years, you can sell it for more money than what you've spent on it while collecting rental income.

The fix-and-flip strategy is also quite common, but you need to gather a little more experience first. In addition, it often needs more initial capital, given you are purchasing a distressed property and have to renovate it. With this strategy, you don't necessarily have to have tenants in mind, but instead, other investors or homeowners. So, cater your renovations to that type of buyer because you will sell it as soon as you've completed renovations. Nonetheless, there are also other things you need to consider, such as your budget for renovation, the financing you want to take on, and so on. You have to fully understand the opportunity, and manage the property and renovations effectively, if you want to make a profit when you sell the property.

Wholesaling is a totally different story. Here, you are the intermediary between the buyer and the seller, and you don't have to purchase the property. However, you do have to look for distressed properties where the owner is very keen to sell the property quickly. Because you don't actually purchase the property yourself, the initial capital required is quite low. Also, the skills used in this strategy are very different from the ones applied in other strategies. For instance, your negotiation skills have to be on point, and your network has to be vast.

House hacking is another viable strategy, especially if you're starting out and don't have a primary property yet. By purchasing a multifamily property, you can rent out the other units while you live in one yourself, which can offset your housing expenses.

KEY TAKEAWAYS

- Estimating an accurate project scope, timeline, and budget often makes or breaks fix-and-flip investments.
- Buy-and-hold properties are the tried-and-true investment strategy for most investors to start building wealth.
- Rental properties allow you to buy a mortgage at a small cost and have other people pay it off for you.
- There are massive tax benefits to real estate investing.

- Wholesaling is a networker's dream, and you don't need a real estate license or money to get started with it.
- House hacking is perfect for young investors or those wanting to drastically reduce or eliminate their personal mortgage. It is by far one of the easiest ways to get started in real estate investing.

FREE GIFT #1

The Only Apartment Investing Book You'll Ever Need: *The Exact Steps To Building Wealth Through Apartment Investing That Anyone Can Follow*

Get your comprehensive guide to apartment investing as a free e-book!

This definitive guide is designed for both beginners and seasoned investors alike. This book walks through the steps to build wealth through apartment investing from finding profitable properties, managing tenants, and maximizing returns, this book can help you gain the knowledge and confidence to succeed in growing your portfolio.

To get instant access this free e-book, scan the QR code below or visit this link: www.readstreetpress.com/realestatebonus1

PART II

HOW TO CLOSE YOUR FIRST DEAL IN 7 SIMPLE STEPS

4

STEP ONE – BUILDING A SOLID FINANCIAL FOUNDATION

I f your personal finances are in good shape, feel free to skip this chapter, as it may not apply to you. However, if you struggle with money, learning good money management skills to invest in real estate and build and maintain wealth is imperative. While this is not a personal finance book, and an in-depth dive into personal money management is outside the scope of this book, we will touch on the basics of what you need to know and do to get started investing in real estate and close your first deal.

Most people are too afraid or embarrassed to admit that their financial situation is not where they feel it should be or want it to be, or that they don't handle their money as well as they could. The good news is there are always ways to improve and change for the better. Everybody makes financial mistakes, and there's no shaming here!

The main reason to check that your finances are in order is to ensure you can be approved for traditional financing should you need it. Banks will only loan you money if they are confident you can repay them. Their team of underwriters assesses your personal finances and the property in question to determine if and how much they are willing to loan to you. The better your finances and track record are, the less risk it is for the bank, and the more likely you are to secure a loan—and secure one with good terms.

While conventional loans are the most common, there are other ways to finance a deal. In fact, you can finance a deal with very little or none of your own money (we'll get to this later in the book), but it is still essential to get your ducks in a row financially. First, you may need or want to use your personal finances at some point in your investing journey. Second, it's easier to find investors and partners who will trust you more when your own finances are in order. Third, good money management habits are extremely important to managing your business and investing finances well. If we don't manage our personal money well, how will we manage a business, where things tend to be much more complicated?

Depending on where you're starting from, it can take a year or more to improve your financial situation, so you must have patience. Trust me—it's worth the time and effort and the wait! So let's get into it.

SETTING GOALS AND REALISTIC EXPECTATIONS

The first step to getting your finances in shape for investing is knowing your goals and setting realistic expectations. If you're looking to invest your own money into your properties, you should have a number in mind of what that is. A good place to start is researching how much the type of property you're looking for is selling for, on average, in the area you want to invest in. Then, as a rule of thumb, you can take 25% of that selling price, which will give you how much money you would need (again, on average, depending on your financing situation) in cash for a down payment. This data will provide you with an estimated amount of money you should aim to have on hand before searching for deals when using traditional financing.

The next step is to take an inventory of your finances, if you don't already know. So many of us are too afraid to look at them to avoid the shame and guilt of our choices. Again, let's set that aside here. No shame or guilt allowed! We must forgive ourselves for our past mistakes and take an objective, almost surgical look at our money situation to fix it and move forward.

So, how much money do you need to get to that 25% cash, if that is your goal? How much can you save monthly to reach that number, and how many months will it take to get there? Can you do something to make extra income to make that goal go faster? Having a realistic plan and timeline will help you stay inspired as you meet your monthly savings goals and keep you motivated to stay the course, knowing there is an end in sight. You are getting closer to it every day.

REDUCING DEBT & IMPROVING YOUR CREDIT SCORE

Reducing personal debt can improve your cash flow and save up cash reserves to invest. Imagine if you didn't have your monthly car, student loan, or mortgage payment (yes, there is a way to reduce this, which we will go into later in the book) and could put that money towards your savings goals. You would progress so much faster!

What if you have multiple forms of debt? How do you choose which to pay first? Make a debt paydown plan. There are two main strategies for how to do this. The standard way is to make all your minimum payments, but then pay extra on the debt with the highest interest rate that costs you the most money. Dave Ramsey's Snowball Method is the second most popular way to pay down debt. Here, you pay all the minimums on your debt. Still, you pay extra money to the debt with the lowest balance first, allowing you to pay off the total debt in full so you can move on, focusing on the next one. This method tends to encourage people as they go along because they feel like they have a win each time they eliminate a debt from their finances.

Let's move on to your credit score. What is it, and why does it matter? Your credit score, or FICO score, is a single number ranging from 300 to 850. It represents your credit risk to lenders. The higher the number, the better you look in the eyes of lenders, as it shows them you are a lower risk. Lenders take your credit score and other information, like your salary, age, assets, etc., to determine if they will lend you money and, if so, how much interest they will charge you. A good credit score is critical because it could save you hundreds of thousands of dollars in interest and be the difference between getting a loan for your investment.

How is a credit score calculated? It's broken down into percentages of specific categories, including 35% payment history (which shows how reliable you are at making payments on time), 30% amounts owed (also known as your credit utilization rate), 15% length of credit history (older accounts are best because they show how reliable you are at making payments), 10% new credit, and 10% types of credit (it's best to have a mix of debt history, including credit card, student loans, car loans, mortgages, etc.).

Don't know what your credit score is? It's extremely easy to check it. There are places like Credit Karma (creditkarma.com) or annualcreditreport.com, where you can get your credit score for free. Sometimes, your bank can provide your score. You can also find your official credit score for a small fee at myfico.com, which tends to be more accurate than the free versions.

What is a good credit score anyway? According to Experian, a major credit bureau whose data comes from the Fair Isaac Corporation (FICO), the quality of credit scores is rated this way:

800+: Exceptional – You'll get approved quickly and for the lowest rates.

740-799: Very Good – You're considered low-risk and will likely get better rates.

670-739: Good – This is where the average American lies. It is regarded as an "acceptable" risk.

580-669: Fair – You'll get mediocre loans with higher interest rates.

579 and below: Poor – If you can get a loan at all, you'll most likely have to put down collateral or a deposit and possibly even have to pay a fee.

So, what should you do if you need better credit? Here are six ways to improve your credit score:

1. **Make payments on time and never miss a payment.** Your payment history is one of the most essential elements of determining your credit score. One way to ensure this happens is by setting up automatic minimum payments where possible (however, if you're going to do this, make sure you don't overdraft your bank account). Paying on time will also help prevent your account from being sent to collections, which would cause your score to dip lower.
2. **Get up to date with all your accounts.** Pay any bills you are behind on to make them current.
3. **Pay down revolving account balances.** Having a high balance on revolving debt like credit cards can hurt your score even if you pay them on time.
4. **Limit the number of new accounts you apply for.** You want to keep hard inquiries on your credit few and far between.
5. **Request higher credit limits.** If your credit limit increases and your balance stays the same, it will automatically decrease your overall credit utilization, improving your credit.
6. **Dispute credit report errors.** Mistakes happen! I personally woke up to my credit score dropping 100+ points one day. I knew I did not do anything for it to drop that drastically, so I immediately reached out to the credit bureau, found out there was an internal error, and they fixed it.

SAVE MORE MONEY

While saving money sounds boring to most people, it is vital to reach the goal of having cash to put into a real estate deal. This doesn't mean you have to stop doing everything you love, but you do need to prioritize your spending. There are multiple approaches to saving money, and we'll focus on the main two.

The first way to increase your savings is to reduce your personal expenses. Many online tools like Empower (empower.com) or Mint (mint.com) can help you keep track of your financial situation and show you precisely how much you are spending in a given category. If there are certain things you don't want to give up, that's fine; quality of life is important, too. However, I'm willing to bet there are things you only care a little about that you are spending much more money on than you'd like. For instance, one expense people are often surprised by is how many subscription services they have that they barely use. So, find out which expenses you care about the least and be ruthless about cutting them out of your budget.

The second way to save money for a down payment is to make more money. Maybe you don't want to reduce your quality of life, or you already have, but it's not moving the needle enough. Fortunately, there are endless ways to make extra money. Whether it be a side hustle, getting a raise, getting a higher-paying job, or selling items or assets you own, you can increase your income and acquire real estate faster.

That's all I'll say on this topic, as most people know how to save money but need to actually do it. Trust me—you can!

KEY TAKEAWAYS

- You must have your finances in good standing to be approved for a conventional loan with a good interest rate. A bad interest rate could cause the deal to lose its cash flow potential, thus turning a good purchasing decision into a bad one.
- Even if you plan to use creative financing to invest in real estate, mastering your personal finances is still necessary, if for nothing else than to have good habits for managing the money involved in your real estate investments.

- Get rid of debt as fast as possible!
- Your credit score is essential, and there are many ways to improve it.
- Saving money doesn't have to hurt, but it needs to happen to reach your goals. Just do it!

5

STEP TWO – FINANCE YOUR FIRST DEAL WITH CONFIDENCE

Real estate cannot be lost or stolen, nor can it be carried away. Purchased with common sense, paid for in full, and managed with reasonable care, it is about the safest investment in the world.

— FRANKLIN D. ROOSEVELT

F inancing your first deal is the second step in the journey of becoming a real estate investor. The first deal you make is always an important one, and one that you want to get right so you can build up confidence. For that to happen, you need to get great financing.

This is exactly what we will be talking about in this chapter: what your options are when it comes to financing your first deal. I'll go through the different loan types you might be able to acquire, how you can find other partners and investors, what other creative financing options are out there, and the different strategies for buying properties when you have no money or bad credit.

DIFFERENT LOAN TYPES

There is a large array of loan types, but this doesn't mean that you will have access to all of them just yet; some of them might not be ideal for you at the moment. But understanding all of them is valuable knowledge, so you know your options.

The most common loans are conventional loans, usually from a bank or other financial institution. These consist of the traditional mortgages many investors take out. They often require you to have quite a high credit score and make large down payments, but their interest rates are some of the best when it comes to financing options. Conventional loans are also a great option if you're following the common buy-and-hold strategy.

There are a few important things that you need to know about conventional loans, including the requirements for down payments, credit score, loan amounts, the terms of the loan, and interest rates. Let's quickly go through them.

The down payment is the initial deposit on the property you want to invest in. This means that you need to pay up front a percentage of the cost of the property, which, on average, is about 20% but can go as low as 3% . There's a lot that goes into the down payment, but typically, the higher the down payment you make, the lower the interest rate you get.

Another thing to take into consideration is credit score requirements. While it's possible for you to get approved for financing with an average credit score—say, around 620—the higher your credit score is, the higher the chances of getting accepted for financing, and the lower your interest rate. Just as a reference, lenders tend to accept a credit score of 660 or above.

The loan amount is how much the bank or financial institution is willing to lend you. Here, the higher the down payment you've advanced, the lower the amount—which is, in many cases, better because it means you don't have to pay as much back to the lender. The loan amount also depends on the property you want to invest in, as well as your credit score. The loan terms for traditional loans are, on average, 30 years; however, between 15 and 20 years is also quite common.

Lastly, interest rates can come in two forms: fixed rate or adjustable rate. As you may have guessed, a fixed-rate loan means you have the same interest rate throughout the term of the loan. On the other hand, adjustable rates can go up or down, depending on the market. However, the most important factor in determining your interest rate is your credit score and your overall credit history.

Another common loan is the Federal Housing Administration (or FHA) loan, which are designed to help first-time buyers or those who have a lower credit score. This can be a suitable loan for your needs. If your credit score is at least 580, you can borrow up to 96.5% of the total cost of the property (Segal, 2019). Therefore, you only really need 3.5% of the down payment to pay upfront. If your score is below 580 and above 500, you can still get financing through FHA, but your minimum down payment has to be at least 10% . Now, FHA is not a lender like a bank is. In these cases, a bank or a mortgage company are still going to be the ones lending you money, but if you get your loan through FHA, they essentially work as guarantors, making it a lot easier for you to get your financing.

There are other types of FHA loans you can look into, such as the home equity conversion mortgage (HECM), which is suitable for those over the age of 62 who want to convert the equity of their property into cash while still remaining homeowners. There's also the FHA 203(k) improvement loan, dedicated to those who want to make renovations to the property, or the FHA energy-efficient mortgage for those who want to renovate the property, but in a way that directly impacts renewable energies or lowers their utility bills.

If you're just starting out in the real estate investing world, hard money loans might not be ideal, but they are an option none-theless. These loans are commonly offered by private lenders or other investors, and they are more suited for short-term invest-ments such as fix-and-flip strategies. Because they come with high interest rates, you want to pay them off as quickly as you can. These types of loans are often based on the value of the property you want to acquire because they often serve as collateral, and unlike a traditional loan, they are not based on your creditworthi-ness. Let's see an example.

It's much faster to get the money with a hard money loan because there's a lot less bureaucracy, and often, you can get the money after 10 days. The average amount lent is usually between 65% and 75% of the value of the property, and the terms vary between six and 18 months. So, say you want to get a hard money loan because you want to buy a fixer-upper for $200,000. The estimation of the renovation costs is $50,000, and you are planning to sell it for $250,000. Say that the lender is lending you 70% of the value of the property after the renovation is done, which is $175,000. There's 11% interest, which means that per month, the lender is making $2,062.50 on interest only each month.

There's also a variant of hard money loans called private money loans. These are often more flexible when it comes to interest rates and repayment terms, but they often depend on the type of relationship you have with the lenders. A popular choice is a seller-financed loan. Here, the seller of the property is the lender and provides you, the buyer, with financing. This means that you need to negotiate directly with the seller, and anything from down payment, repayment terms, or interest rates also has to be discussed with the seller. I will go through these types of loans in more detail later in the book.

There are other less common loans, such as veteran affairs, or VA loans, which are exclusively for veterans or active-duty service members; United States Department of Agriculture loans, or USDA loans, designed to promote rural home ownership; portfolio loans, which are offered by credit unions or banks, but are not sold to secondary mortgage markets; or commercial loans if you want to find financing for commercial real estate, like retail spaces or office buildings. Commercial loans can be quite different from the more conventional loans in terms of interest rates, for instance. They usually cover not only capital expenditure but also operational costs that the company may have. These loans are often designed for small businesses to be able to pay for their basic operational needs, like buying supplies or funding payroll. Often, you are required to have collateral, frequently property, in case you default on your payments. We can look at these types of loans as short-term funding for businesses that are struggling to get started, and the terms vary between 3-5 years. The interest rates also vary between 7% and 8% .

Choosing the perfect loan for you is critical, but it also depends on numerous aspects, like your financial status, your plan, the sort of property you want to invest in, and so on. You must also consider down payments, interest rates, repayment periods, and everything else I've discussed. As usual, speaking with a professional, such as a mortgage broker or a financial counselor, will help you understand your best options.

FINDING PARTNERS AND INVESTORS

Choosing suitable partners or investors is critical in the real estate world, as they have the capacity to drastically change your trajectory in the industry. These connections not only allow you to diversify your portfolio and boost your funds, but also enable you to take on larger projects to improve your professional background. Because of this, acquiring the information and abilities needed to choose the perfect partner is essential.

There isn't always a need to locate partners or investors, especially if you're just starting out and have the funds and knowledge to take that initial step, but you must be able to recognize when you do need these people. Typically, you would seek investors and partners in two situations: when you wish to grow your firm, and when you want resources or skills in an area where you lack experience. When it comes to growing your business, you will most likely discover that your financial resources alone will not be sufficient to progress to greater initiatives; therefore, partnering might be a fantastic solution. Here, partners and investors can also contribute experience, contacts, and additional resources. For instance, if you want to start exploring fix-and-flip strategies, knowing someone with a background or skill in remodeling can come in handy.

DIFFERENT TYPES OF INVESTORS AND PARTNERS

Depending on your individual goals, you have a variety of possibilities for choosing investors and partners. One example of a widely desired partnership is an equity partner, who injects funds into your investment in exchange for an interest in its ownership. The extent to which they are involved in day-to-day activities may vary depending on your agreement. Private investors, sometimes known as silent partners, take a somewhat different strategy. They offer funds without actively participating in the project but expect a return on their investment, which might take the form of a percentage of earnings or interest payments.

Joint ventures are something you might want to consider, and they are quite common in the industry. Here, you'd partner up with one or more individuals or companies that have the same goals as you. One thing that you have to take into account is the bureaucratic side, which is quite a bit more than doing it alone. This is because when creating a joint venture, you have to specify the roles each individual or entity is responsible for, what their exact responsibilities are, and the financial arrangements between each partner.

In the past few years, a different type of investment has become popular: crowd-funding platforms. These platforms can be websites that connect investors within the real estate industry, and as an investor, you can make small contributions to join a large real estate project. Relatedly, there are real estate investment clubs, which are similar to crowd-funding platforms but have been going on for way longer. There are usually local or online real estate investment clubs where you can network with other real estate investors.

BUILDING RELATIONSHIPS

Knowing how to build relationships is crucial in this business, as I've stated before. When it comes to networking, there are many ways you can do it. For instance, as I've mentioned above, crowd-funding platforms or real estate investment clubs are a great way to start.

However, you don't necessarily have to join a club to do this. All you have to do is pay attention to any real estate industry event, conferences, or simple meet-ups happening in your local area. Here, not only do investors attend, but you can network with a large array of different professionals in the industry, such as developers, lawyers, realtors, and so on. Again, online platforms such as real estate forums can be a great way to network with other professionals, have discussions, or share your experiences and expertise.

CREATING A PARTNER'S PROPOSAL

When it's time to approach a potential partner or even an investor, your proposal has to be clear, and you have to have everything detailed properly so there's no confusion in the future. You should, for instance, add an outline of the investment opportunity, roles, risks, or expected returns. You also have to come up with a risk mitigation strategy and show that you are committed to the project. Lastly, make sure you add any financial projections to show the potential of the investment.

Now, all of this has to be bound by law, so you need to draft legal agreements. There are two main legal agreements you have to know about. If you are seeking to bring in a partner, then a partnership agreement is what you are looking to draft. This is a way to formalize the arrangement, and the document should have a clear description of the roles of each partner, their ownership shares, their responsibilities, and any other things you might find important.

The other legal agreement is a private placement memorandum, or PPM, and should be done when you're seeking funds from a private investor. This document should disclose important information about the potential investment and other relevant things. In both of these cases, you should have a real estate lawyer draft these documents, and they should be rectified by the other party's lawyer, too.

Whether you are seeking a partner or an investor, communication is important, especially in the case of a partner because they tend to be more involved in the operations of the investment. You should be looking for open and transparent communication to ensure that any agreement you and the other party sign complies with any laws or regulations in place. Bringing in a financial advisor might also be important because they have experience with any type of tax implications the new agreement might bring.

To make sure you're on the same page, ensure your goals align with your partner's or investor's. At this point, you should also mention the strategies you want to apply and your risk tolerance. Before signing any agreements, it's important to discuss an exit plan with your partner or investor. For instance, how will the partnership or investment be dissolved?

Finding the right partner can be a hurdle, but to set that up, you need to come up with a great strategy before you even think about taking an approach. Once that is out of the way and you've found your partner, you have to know that all parties are equally committed to the project. I'm highlighting this because it often happens that one of the parties is not as involved in the process, which usually doesn't end well.

Altogether, you have to keep in mind that this is something you are likely to seek in the future as your career progresses. So, while this might not cross your mind at this point in your career, networking from the beginning will allow you these opportunities in the future, so when the time comes, you don't have to rush into getting the right contacts.

CREATIVE FINANCING OPTIONS

We've already talked about some of the most common finance approaches you can get, which I highly recommend before utilizing more creative financing options. This is because creative options are often not as favorable as traditional methods, but that doesn't mean they are always bad. Many of them depend on your unique circumstances, and sometimes the only way to get finance for certain projects is through these creative finances. Let's look at some of these options.

One of the most common creative financing options is leasing. This method involves leasing a property and adding the opportunity to purchase it at a later date at a specific price. This allows you to generate revenue while not being fully committed (monetarily) to the investment. It's a great way to understand if this investment can potentially work if you go all in. It also allows you to have more time for traditional financing.

Another option you might want to consider is something called "subject-to-financing," where you take over an existing mortgage on a property, but leave the property under the seller's name. The benefit is that you keep the current mortgage the seller has without making a new one, potentially not increasing the mortgage on the property. This also means that you may have a reduced down payment or no down payment at all.

Another option is the seller-carryback mortgage, which happens when the seller provides you with a part of the financing and acts as a secondary lender (besides the primary lender). Often, this primary mortgage comes from traditional financing, such as from a bank, but simultaneously, the seller carries the second mortgage. There are benefits here, such as reducing the down payment for the property and making it a lot easier for you to qualify for finance. The hardest part of this approach is finding a seller who is willing to do this.

A wraparound mortgage is similar to the one described above, but it involves preserving the existing mortgage and adding an extra layer of financing, with payments sent to the seller who is paying the original mortgage. This enables you to purchase a new investment without having to pay off your previous mortgage.

Cross-collateralization, which isn't as prevalent as others on this list, consists of using one of your own properties to acquire financing for numerous others. This maximizes your leverage, but also significantly raises your risk because your property is being used as collateral.

There's another way to find a creative financing solution if you have a self-directed IRA or a 401(k). Using this strategy offers a few tax advantages, but you'd be using your retirement account to invest in property, which may have some consequences, as you might imagine.

Then there's the seller leaseback, which encompasses a seller staying in the property as a tenant after you've purchased the property. This is a great strategy if you're looking to generate rental income from the get-go.

With all of this said, creative financing options are any type of financing you can arrange that is not within traditional financing. This means that many of these creative options are customized for your and the seller's needs. The best way to reach a customized deal is by sitting down with the seller and another investor and finding ways to structure the deal that benefit each party involved.

There are plenty of things and angles you can use to reach a deal that are not necessarily based on any of the options I've talked about in this section. Things like profit-sharing agreements, various purchase options, or deferred payments are all possible as long as every party is happy. Despite that, due diligence is the way to go when approaching such deals and gain leverage when negotiating, as well as hiring professionals to guide you through these negotiations.

STRATEGIES FOR BUYING REAL ESTATE WITH LITTLE MONEY OR BAD CREDIT

There are numerous ways you can invest in real estate and start your career, even if you don't have enough money for a down payment, or if you have bad credit. Wholesaling is one of them since, as you know, these sorts of properties are typically priced below market value for a variety of reasons, including those mentioned earlier.

Another technique that might offer you more time to locate cash is to lease a home with the option to buy it later at a certain price. Also, when you don't have enough money to invest in real estate, you might use partnerships or the seller's financing. Alternatively, you can employ certain unconventional financing methods, such as subject-to-finance or wraparound mortgages.

There are other strategies we haven't talked about yet. For instance, you can rent out a spare room you have in your current property. This way, you can generate income and use it for potential investments down the road. Alternatively, looking at local government programs is a good idea since these might offer down payment assistance or low-interest loans.

I think that the best way for you to find the best possible financing strategy when you don't have enough money or your credit score is not ideal is to explore creative financing resources. Go to real estate investment clubs or simply network in any way because you might be able to find many other opportunities. Owner financing websites can help you find properties with owner financing options, or you can go to community banks, credit unions, or any other small financial institution because they tend to be more flexible when offering loans and mortgages.

Being able to finance your first deal requires substantial planning and thought before you act on it. It's how you can set up your career for great heights and become a successful real estate investor. Everything we've seen here, from the different types of loans, their advantages and disadvantages, and how they relate to your financial goals, is crucial, as is your understanding of the current market and its cycle. While you should always consider traditional loans, creative strategies might work better for you in certain unique circumstances.

One thing you have total control over is networking, creating partnerships, and leveraging those partnerships to lead you to better opportunities. Building relationships with other professionals is a big part of the job of a real estate investor, and you should get to know professionals from other backgrounds if you want to increase the chances of great opportunities coming your way.

It's especially important to build relationships with other investors so you can find more and better opportunities in your career. Networking is a big part of the job. Here, you can go to conferences and real estate events and meet other investors face to face. You can also join online groups to meet online.

If you're looking for partners and think you've found the right one, it's important that you craft a strong partner's proposal. This agreement includes legal requirements that should always be drafted by your attorney or at least verified by them. Such a proposal should outline the tasks each partner has, any risks associated with them, financial projections, risk mitigation, and so on.

If you find yourself with bad credit or limited funds and still want to invest, there are certain options you can go for. Wholesaling, for instance, is a great way to get into the real estate industry without investing too much initially. A lease with the option to buy is another great opportunity, allowing you to rent a property with the agreement that you will purchase it at a later date. In real estate investing, where there's a will, there's a way.

Now that we've talked about the different ways you can finance your first deal, in the next chapter, we'll discuss how to get preapproved if you're going the standard traditional financing route. Then, we'll find your first deal.

KEY TAKEAWAYS

- Finding financing for your first deal is a crucial step to starting your career as a real estate investor.
- Conventional loans: The most common loan mortgages are usually from banks that require a down payment and a high credit score.
- FHA loans: These loans are great for first-time buyers or those with a low credit score.
- Seller-financed loans: The seller finances the loan, and you can essentially come up with your own terms between you and the lender.
- Hard money loans: These loans are best used for short-term strategies such as fix-and-flip, as they tend to have high interest rates.
- Private money loans: Loans offered by private investors instead of banks and other financial institutions. They offer you more flexibility when it comes to the terms of the agreement.

- Other loans, like USDA or VA loans, can be used in very specific circumstances.
- Finding other investors and partners to work with can change the trajectory of your portfolio.
- Equity partners, or investors that inject capital into the investment and take part in the ownership, or private investors, which simply provide funds, are the most common types of investment partners.
- Crowd-funding platforms can be a great way to find other investors or people to partner with for joint ventures.
- Creative financing can be the key to unlock tremendous opportunities that most investors miss.

FREE GIFT #2

Free Bonus Chapter About Creative Financing: Don't let your bank account stop you from your dreams!

Learn the basics of seller financing, lease options, and cash-out financing to help you find creative options to acquire more properties! What are some of the pitfalls to avoid? Find out in this exclusive chapter!

To get instant access this free e-book, scan the QR code below or visit this link: www.readstreetpress.com/realestatebonus2

6

STEP THREE – FIND YOUR FIRST DEAL

Buy on the fringe and wait. Buy land near a growing city! Buy real estate when other people want to sell. Hold what you buy!

— JOHN JACOB ASTOR

Now that you know how real estate investing works, the different types of real estate, and the most common strategies you can use, you have to find your first deal. There are a few steps that you need to follow.

The first thing we'll be looking at in this chapter is how you can get preapproved for financing. You need to first obtain financing for your property purchase before you can move on to the next steps. Then, we'll explore how to get an investor-friendly realtor who is more than happy to work with you and help you find a deal.

Keep in mind, however, that finding a deal with an agent is not always a sure thing. If this is the case, you might have to look at properties yourself, which is something that we will also cover in this chapter. This should be the third step when looking for a property to invest in.

GETTING PREAPPROVED FOR FINANCING

Your very first step toward securing finance is getting preapproved. Preapproval has many benefits, especially for the seller, as they will see you as a serious investor. It will also help you determine your budget and, in turn, narrow down the strategies you will want to use.

There can be a little confusion between preapproval and prequalification. They might sometimes be used interchangeably, but they are different things. If you are prequalified, it means the lender has made an informal assessment of your finances. It's faster to do it, and it's definitely a great start, but it's not nearly as strong as a statement as preapproval. On that note, preapproval involves a more rigorous evaluation where the lender checks your employment, your credit history, your income, and many other things to fully understand your financial situation.

As I've said, once you get preapproved, it essentially means that your budget is clear – the letter you receive specifies how much money the lender will lend you, which, in turn, helps you figure out what properties will be in your price range. Leveraging preapproval during your negotiations is perhaps the best advantage it will give you, and while it doesn't 100% guarantee a loan, it's as close as it can get to an approval for a loan or mortgage.

STEPS TO GET PREAPPROVED

When you are preparing to apply for a loan and get preapproved, you have to look for a lender. If this is all new to you, larger banks might be easier to deal with, as well as mortgage companies or credit unions. However, they are far from being the only lenders.

Once you've found a lender, you will need to provide all the necessary documentation for preapproval, which usually involves bank statements, any information about your liabilities and debts, employment history, and income verification documents (pay stubs, W-2 forms, or tax returns if you're self-employed). As you know, lenders will do a credit check on you to find out your creditworthiness, and here, your credit score will be important.

66

Once you've satisfied all of those requirements, you need to complete your loan application. This process once again requires you to give the lender other financial information as well as personal information. The lender will then review all of the documents and assess them. If everything's good, you will get a conditional approval, where you will see the maximum loan amount you can get, though this approval is still pending additional documentation and a property appraisal. This is because the lender will need an appraisal of the property you want to purchase to make sure that the property value checks out with the loan amount. Once that is done and everything's right, you will get your final approval for the loan, and you will also get your preapproval letter.

One important thing to take into account is that preapproval letters have an expiration date, so make sure you find a property during the allotted time. If you let the letter expire, you will have to go through the whole process again. Also, while getting preapproved is a great thing, you have to keep managing your finances properly throughout the property-buying process. This means not making big financial changes like changing jobs, buying something expensive, or even taking out a personal loan. Taking these actions might make the lender reconsider your preapproval.

FINDING AN INVESTOR-FRIENDLY REALTOR

An experienced realtor who is on board with working with real estate investors can be a great asset, especially when you're just starting out in this industry. However, if you haven't previously met anyone with those characteristics, it might take a while before you do. This is not to say that you can't go out there and find one, of course. In this section, I will first highlight the benefits a real estate agent can bring to you.

An experienced real estate agent has vast knowledge of investment and therefore understands all the common strategies I've talked about here. Their expertise goes beyond the common residential property purchase, as they also understand market trends, rental income analysis, property types, and more. Most importantly, they can give you excellent advice that is tailored to your own goals. In addition, they can find better properties that align with your needs a lot faster, they have a much better understanding of the local market, their negotiation skills are sharp and can help you tremendously, and they have a great network of resources available to them.

Now, this is all great, but how can you find a good realtor? The first thing you should do is to ask for referrals. This essentially means asking your fellow real estate investors for recommendations, as they might know someone who works with investors. But you shouldn't always take their word for it, and you might want to conduct some interviews. After all, you're looking for a partnership where the realtor also benefits. In these interviews, you can ask them about the type of experience they have, their knowledge of the local market, and so on. You should also check their credentials to make sure they align with what they say, or even check their portfolio.

Once you've found your realtor, you need to know how to work with them. Here, you want to first define your investment goals for them so they can offer you the best properties they have that align with those goals. You should also discuss your expectations when it comes to choosing a property and doing market analysis. Remember that your real estate agent has been in the market for a long time, so perhaps they can link you with other professionals so you can create a team of experts. I'm talking about real estate attorneys, property inspectors, contractors, appraisers, and so on —anything that can make your investment process easier.

As with everything, clear communication is essential, so you should communicate with your realtor on a regular basis and discuss any investment opportunities that might have appeared.

SEARCHING FOR POTENTIAL PROPERTIES

Before you get out there and start looking for properties, you have to make your goals clear, have a great knowledge of the market, understand your risk mitigation, and know the type of property you want to purchase. Only then should you start looking for a property.

The first place I like to look is at online real estate platforms. I'm talking about Realtor.com, Zillow, and Multiple Listing Service (MLS), not only because they host many different properties, but you can also filter those properties to find the one for you. Again, make sure you use your realtor during your search, especially if they have knowledge of the local market. They can give you many different resources and even give you access to off-market listings.

If you haven't established your network, do it as fast as you can. To make this easier, you can attend local real estate investment groups, for instance, where networking is the main thing they do, and where you will find a variety of professionals in the real estate business.

Alternatively, you can send marketing emails to property owners in the area you want to invest in to show them your interest in buying their property. There are also auctions you can attend, which offer great opportunities for below-market prices.

Lastly, remember the wholesaler strategy? Even if you're not following that particular strategy, you can contact wholesalers because they often have access to distressed properties you might consider buying.

PROPERTY DUE DILIGENCE AND EVALUATION

Before you even do your due diligence on a desired property, you should already have your budget more or less defined. That means, by this point, you already have a list of properties you can invest in. Doing your due diligence and evaluation will narrow this list down even further.

Inspecting the property is the first thing you have to do, followed by a close examination of the local market. During the inspection, you need to pay attention to the conditions of the property, so here, hiring an expert is a necessity. When it comes to analyzing the local market, consider recent sales, appreciation of local properties, or expected rental income, among other things. At the same time, performing the financial analysis is important so you can understand your return on investment (ROI), cash flow, and other important metrics.

Also, research any regulatory and legal subjects to make sure the property you're thinking of purchasing complies with all the local zoning and regulatory requirements. While doing that, it's always a good idea to research the property's history, like past sales, past ownership, or any legal issues past owners had. This is to make sure you are prepared if any of those issues arise at some point.

All of this information can be gathered through your due diligence, which proves vital when you reach the negotiation phase. At this point, you can leverage any findings you've unearthed, like repairs that need to be fixed, which raises the issue of whether you or the owner should pay for them. If you're the one paying for them, make sure you negotiate the price of the property to a lower number so you can factor in the expenses of those repairs.

Due diligence is almost always a long process, so it's important that you are patient and don't try to rush things. Not every property you see will be a good fit. Keep that in mind and be mindful of making the best possible decision every step of the way.

Let's go through an example of doing due diligence. Let's say you want to purchase a single-family property, and it's listed at $150,000. It's a great location, just outside a major city in a suburban area. At this point, you've found that the recent appreciation rate is 4%, and the local real estate market is relatively stable. That particular area has been built recently, so it's attracting quite a few professionals and has a growing job market. Upon inspecting the property, you notice there are some minor repairs to be made that total $6,000 (as an estimate). You've done your financial analysis and compared the property to similar properties in the neighborhood, and you expect to generate around $1,800 a month through rental income. You also find that the expected annual expenses, including maintenance, property insurance, and property taxes, go for around $3,500.

You get financing by putting down 20%, which is $30,000, and for the rest, you get a mortgage loan at 3.5% over 30 years.

So far, this is what you have:

- Annual rental income is $21,600 ($1,800 x 12)
- Annual expenses are expected to be $3,500
- Mortgage payment: $538.85 monthly

This is assuming the property complies with local zoning and regulations, the title comes back clear, there are no environmental issues, and all the legal procedures were done correctly.

NETWORKING

As mentioned, networking is one of the most important things you can do in the real estate industry. Its focus is to connect with other people, and those connections will eventually help you become successful in the long term. Having a broad network of connections is almost invaluable, but not only do you need to connect with other professionals in your industry, but in other industries as well, because you don't know what challenges you might come across.

I've highlighted the value of networking in past chapters. From the network you build, you can get advice, increase your chances of getting a good deal, or even find another investor to form a partnership. But we haven't yet discussed how you can find and form these connections.

Here, it's important that you apply some networking strategies. For example, attending business events is a great way to start, but there are plenty of other things you can do. You should leverage today's digital age and try to find communities on online forums or social media platforms. Alternatively, you can join your local real estate association, which often holds monthly meetings that might be beneficial to you if you're just starting out. Any of these strategies will allow you to share your thoughts, ask questions, and, of course, connect with other like-minded professionals. You can also do a mentorship, where someone with experience in the field teaches you how the industry works.

Although the most important thing to focus on is trying to build long-term relationships with these professionals and eventually form partnerships with them, this is not as easy as it might seem. A true networking connection has to be a relationship where you give and take; that's the only way to form strong relationships. Constant communication is also vital, as is being reliable when your network needs you and asks for your help.

This doesn't necessarily mean you should only work with one contractor or realtor, for instance. But you should prioritize your relationships while trying not to burn bridges with anyone. Having a diverse network will allow you to reach your goals faster; after all, you can't expect that your preferred realtor or contractor will always be available. Furthermore, the more diverse your network, the more exposure you get to other professionals and other industries, as well as strategies and perspectives that might lead to unique opportunities.

As you can see, networking is a critical part of being a real estate investor. To continually increase your network, you have to engage with other professionals on a regular basis and make an effort to always try to get to know more people. You also need to provide them with value and nurture your relationship with them so they become long-term partnerships. The time you spend making these connections is an investment in your business; it's impossible to be successful in the industry if you don't meet other people and partner up with them. You need other professionals to help you, and in return, you need to help them.

What we've been discussing throughout the chapter is the very first step for you to take to establish yourself as a real estate investor. Finding your first deal might make you a little nervous at first, but it doesn't have to be that way. Before that, you need to find finance, which often means getting at least preapproved for a loan. When that is done, you will have a much clearer understanding of what your budget might be, which will allow you to strengthen your position as an investor in the eyes of a seller. You should also try to find an investor-friendly realtor who can point out many opportunities you wouldn't have come across on your own and find the perfect investment for you more easily.

This doesn't mean you shouldn't do your due diligence; in fact, this step is essential so you can narrow down the list of potential properties you might invest in. Lastly, networking and building relationships are as important as investing and doing due diligence because they will allow you to take advantage of more diverse opportunities.

KEY TAKEAWAYS

- Getting preapproved for financing is the first step to finding your first deal if you are aiming to do traditional funding. It shows sellers you are serious about purchasing the property and helps you determine your budget.
- An investor-friendly realtor can give you an edge in your search due to their better understanding of the local market, market cycles, and trends. They also may have access to listings you don't.
- Having clear goals and criteria of what you're looking for in a property is key to closing on your first deal as fast as possible and being efficient with time.
- Online platforms, email marketing, direct mail, and local investment groups are all ways to find good deals.
- Inspections are critical to know if you have to do any major repairs that would impact your financial analysis or overall plan for the property.
- Networking is always a good idea for any investor to keep a pulse on their local market and find properties before they're even listed.

FREE GIFT #3

Investor Networking Guide: It's all about who you know so get networking!

Real estate investing can be difficult, that is why you should not do it alone! From investor friendly real estate agents to potential business partners, it is important to have a team of individuals you can count when you need an extra boost. In this guide you'll learn about the importance of networking and provides practical advice on how to build and maintain valuable relationships within the industry.

To get instant access this free e-book, scan the QR code below or visit this link: www.readstreetpress.com/realestatebonus3

7

STEP FOUR – BECOME AN EXPERT AT DEAL ANALYSIS & DUE DILIGENCE

Buy land, they aren't making any more of it.

— MARK TWAIN

Analyzing your deals is the fourth step to finding and closing on your first deal. The process used to analyze deals is called due diligence. I've mentioned it here several times, but in this chapter, we will delve deeper into what due diligence entails and how you can hone the necessary skills to perform it properly.

We will also be talking about other things related to due diligence, such as how you can evaluate the condition of a property, how to assess different market conditions, how to make better decisions based on the data you've gathered from your due diligence, and when you should leverage all this information into action when it comes to making a deal.

CONDUCTING DUE DILIGENCE

As you now know, doing exhaustive due diligence is the most efficient way to assess your investment options. This approach entails a wide variety of steps and consists of a thorough review of potential investment assets. While there are various objectives for due diligence, the main focus should be risk reduction, followed by making well-informed decisions and ensuring your assets match your financial goals. However, due diligence also serves as a strategy for verifying the property's pricing. All the data acquired during due diligence offers you additional bargaining power and make certain that all legal duties are carried out.

Let's explore the main points of due diligence, starting with property inspection. While I'll go in-depth on this subject later in this chapter, you have to hire a qualified inspector to check the property. This professional will then assess the property's structural integrity and the functionality of all its systems, including electrical, plumbing, and HVAC, just to name a few. You will also want to verify the title of the property, which is also known as a title search. This is simply a way to determine who actually owns the property and if there are any legal disputes that could potentially affect your investment.

After that, you want to make a financial analysis of the property, but we will explore this particular aspect later in this chapter. In sum, you will have to crunch some numbers like NOI, ROI, or rental demand to ensure the financials align with your goals.

Then there's the market analysis, which entails doing research on your local area to figure out appreciation trends, rental demand, and other market conditions that might have an effect on your potential investment. You might also have to do an environmental assessment, especially if you're investing in commercial property. This is to know if there are any environmental hazards or any other type of contamination on the property that might affect the tenants, the public, or both. While doing this assessment and considering the regulatory and legal compliance, it's crucial to understand if safety regulations have been put in place or if there are any violations of permits.

Due diligence also involves researching the property's history. This doesn't only mean looking at past ownership, but also any structural issues that might have happened in the past. Also, when applying to get preapproved, you have to get a professional appraisal done because this might help you draw contingencies on the potential deal to protect your interests.

One thing that many new real estate investors are not aware of is the time constraint to conduct due diligence. This timeframe is often outlined in the purchase agreement you sign with the seller. Due diligence not an easy process to go through on your own, so it's vital that you bring in experts to help you out. For instance, hiring property inspectors, appraisers, real estate attorneys, and any other professionals might be useful because they can provide you with invaluable insights into your potential property. Also, don't forget to look at local construction trends, local rental trends, and local large businesses, as well as tax breaks on properties in the area.

Once you've finished these steps, you'll have a wealth of data to guide your decisions and finesse your negotiations. Know that acquiring this information does not bind you to a purchase; in fact, that's why due diligence is performed. If the information you've acquired recommends it, you can negotiate additional conditions. Always keep in mind that your investment selection should be in line with your investing goals and risk tolerance.

Due diligence is a non-negotiable stage in the property investment process. It protects your interests by ensuring you make sound choices and protecting you from any future troubles. By evaluating a property's physical condition, financial feasibility, market context, and legal compliance, you improve your decision-making and dramatically increase your chances of success in the real estate investment sector. Let me give you a few checklists on the due diligence you might want to conduct.

When looking at financial due diligence, make sure you go through:

- Vacancy tax deductions
- Tax and insurance liabilities
- Rent variability
- Gross rental income
- History of rent variations and tenant breakdown

- Operating expenses

When looking at property and land due diligence, ensure that you go through:

- Costs required to repurpose the building (if necessary)
- Engineer and architect inspection
- Land survey
- Environmental rating

Looking at legal due diligence, remember to go through:

- History of ownership
- Legal encumbrances related to the property
- Any outstanding legal obligations currently on the property
- Building control, environmental, zoning, and any other relevant regulations
- Access rights

Altogether, the main reasons for due diligence are illiquidity, cyclicality, and understanding if the property is fit for purpose. Let me explain.

As you know, real estate is one of the most illiquid assets you can invest in. This means that if you were in need of money (as in cash), selling your property would take quite some time for you to see that cash. Once you sign the contract on a property acquisition, this often means you are tying yourself up for quite a few years (unless it is a fix-and-flip strategy, but still). Due diligence is also a great tool to understanding the cycles of the industry, as this particular industry is highly cyclical. This means that when you're in a good cycle, properties seem like a great investment, but not so much when the economy goes through a bad cycle.

Lastly, fit for purpose simply means ensuring that the property you're acquiring is suitable for the strategy you want to pursue.

EVALUATING PROPERTY CONDITIONS

An important aspect when conducting due diligence is how to evaluate the property you're potentially investing in. This often means evaluating the physical conditions of the property, such as its structural integrity, to ensure everything is fine and aligned with your goals.

The benefits of doing this are to reduce your risks, help you draw up a financial plan, and make your investment more suitable and aligned with your financial goals. Due diligence also gives you leverage when it comes to negotiating prices, as you will know exactly what the upsides and downsides of the property are.

As I've mentioned, the structural integrity of the property is one of the most important factors to consider when conducting due diligence. You should hire an inspector to look at the property's foundation, including its walls, roofs, and floors. They look at any cracks, signs of water damage, or anything else that might become an issue later on. But structural integrity is not the only thing inspectors will be looking at; they also look at the property's systems, such as HVAC, electrical systems, and plumbing.

The problem with not finding these issues before purchasing the property is that fixing them takes a small fortune. You also will not be able to rent the property while there is work going on. Often, inspectors also look at the interior and exterior of the property to detect any signs of mold, pests, water intrusion, or anything else that might damage the property going forward. As I've said before, inspectors thoroughly conduct inspections of roofs and gutters and check the condition of the shingles for any signs of leaks.

Hiring a qualified and licensed property inspector is your best shot at identifying any of those issues before purchasing the property. They are professionals, and that's what they do. Years of experience have given them the insights to look closer at things we wouldn't even notice that might eventually become a problem. Furthermore, after their inspection, they give you a detailed report with recommendations on how you can act upon any of the issues they've identified.

With the professional inspection done, you are better informed to add any contingencies to the purchase agreement and protect yourself better. This simply means adding clauses that might allow you to renegotiate some of the terms of the contract or even walk away from the deal if you can't find a consensus with the seller. For example, after you've received the inspector's report, you'll estimate the costs of fixing everything. At this point, you can renegotiate with the seller on how things can be fixed, if they want to do it themselves, or if they would rather lower the price of the property and have you fix any issues yourself.

Without the keen eye of a professional inspector, you may not be able to notice all the issues happening with the property, which means potentially paying for repairs yourself down the line. If, for instance, you agree with the seller that they do the repairs before the purchase is done, and they haven't completed them, one of the contingencies you might have added is to walk away from the deal. This way, you won't have lost a lot of money.

Before the inspector comes in, you can also do your own evaluation. It won't be as thorough, but it might be important. As you start checking some of the most evident issues the property might have, add them to your list of things to repair. The first thing you have to do is to understand your priorities. For instance, you shouldn't think about installing new light fittings if the wiring is not properly done and it's dangerous. Or, if the property is not secure enough, you shouldn't even think about adding any expensive fixtures. It's always best to take it from the top, and I mean this literally – starting with the roof. However, don't put yourself in a dangerous situation by climbing a ladder to get to the roof (that's the inspector's job). Instead, you can get a pair of binoculars to examine the roof more closely and look for any evident damage. If you can't see it from the street, you can always ask a neighbor to let you onto their property for a better vantage point.

Also, get into the loft or attic so you can better inspect the roof from the inside. Here, you can look for water stains on the timbers. Ideally, wait for heavy rain and check it so you can be sure that there are no issues when it rains heavily. There should also be ventilators on the roof slope, along the eaves, or in the gable walls.

If there are not, you have to make a note of it because poor ventilation will create mold. If there's a chimney in the property, make sure to inspect it for cracks or other damage, as these are the most exposed parts of the property.

Also, check the yard if the property has one. You should be assessing the condition of the fences, the roof of the shed (if there is one), lighting on any paths, or trees that might need trimming.

You should also check the downpipes or gutters for any blockages. If there are water stains on the inside or outside of the walls, this can tell you where there might have been some water damage from blockages. You can see this damage better when it rains. Moreover, if there's quite a bit of woodwork around the house, such as balconies, door frames, and so on, look for rotten wood (wood is especially exposed to weather conditions when facing west and north).

You should not only look for ventilation in the roof, but in the entire house. If the property is built on exposed bricks, you can look for air bricks, but most properties should have grilles built into the walls (usually above ground level). Sufficient air circulation is vital to fight mold and damp conditions, so make sure there is enough ventilation and none of the grilles is blocked. If the property has wood floors, just by walking on them, you might feel them sinking lightly. This often means the joints have rotted, so it's best to get them repaired, as their tendency is to get worse over time and more expensive.

After the property evaluation is done, you can make better-informed decisions on how to move ahead with the deal. You will have a much clearer idea of how the property might align with your financial goals and if any repairs are coming out of your pocket or that of the seller. This step in your due diligence is crucial to ensuring that you get a good deal. One of the jobs of a real estate investor is to be well informed about their potential deals and maximize their returns, as well as mitigate their investment risks.

ASSESSING MARKET CONDITIONS

Assessing market conditions is also essential when doing due diligence. Essentially, this process is about analyzing the real estate market in a broad way, but in the area that you want to invest in. Understanding market conditions is another way for you to make an informed decision and to make sure this aligns with your financial goals.

There are many benefits to doing an assessment of the local market conditions. For instance, it allows you to assess the level of risk associated with your potential investment. Here, you will be looking at the fluctuations of supply and demand, market volatility, or any other economic factors that can have an effect on the value of the property now or in the future.

As you know, whatever affects the value of the property also affects your rental income. A market assessment also allows you to perfect your investment strategy. I mean that depending on the market conditions, you might opt for a different strategy than you first envisioned. Also, as you know, different market conditions might be more or less favorable to the different strategies.

Assessing the market conditions gives you a greater understanding of the real cost of your investment, protecting you from overpaying for an investment property. It also aids in the development of an exit strategy; for example, if the market is now better for selling than for purchasing, you may choose to postpone your purchase until more favorable buying conditions happen.

Multiple elements should be considered while assessing market conditions. A full assessment requires things such as an evaluation of local market dynamics, which includes a review of data such as vacancy rates, property valuation trends, and local rental demand. Also, the strength or weakness of the real estate market is highly linked to economic measures such as income growth, economic stability, and employment rates in the area.

One of the most important elements is the balance between property supply and demand in the area in question. This aspect too demands a thorough examination. For example, a scarcity of available rental properties usually results in a rise in rental revenue, whereas an oversupply usually results in a drop in rental prices. The relationship between property demand and availability is certainly an important aspect in the context of property acquisition or selling; however, it is critical not to neglect the impact of mortgage rates, given they are one of the key drivers influencing property purchase or sale options.

You have to consider seasonal trends as well as your property's location. Let me give you an example: if you have a property near a tourist location and you rent it out, you are likely to expect an increase in rental income during the holiday season, right? However, you have to factor in other things, such as zoning and regulatory changes, that might have an impact on the property's value. The best way to get a sense of the prices and values of surrounding properties is to look at recent comparable sales, also known as "comps." These can be really helpful when trying to figure out the value of your property. Not only that, you also have to understand real estate cycles and figure out if you're in a seller's or buyer's market, as this can have a significant impact on the value and price of properties. Let's break this down.

Starting with the local economics, there's quite a bit to look into. One of these is employment trends. Doing your research here will tell you how healthy the market is currently and in the future. In a simple way, if people have jobs, they will be able to afford rent. If there are no local jobs or there's quite a bit of unemployment, people will often move away from the area. The best way to get concrete numbers is through the Bureau of Labor Statistics as well as the local chamber of commerce. You should also look into the net migration in the local area. This includes various parameters, such as household income, population growth, and the age distribution of the population.

Essentially, you have to look at the demographics of the area to understand the demand for different types of properties. For instance, if, looking at population growth, you find out that people are moving away from the area, this would mean that it would be harder for you to rent the property. If there's a large university nearby, maybe looking at properties that students are more likely to rent might give you an advantage. Looking at net migration and demographics in general has a massive impact on the demand in that particular market and even on the appreciation of the property. On the other hand, if the population grows, demand for properties grows as well, which helps with renting the property and increases the value and appreciation of the property.

Still, within the local economy, you should look at industry diversification. If the local market has enough diversification (or a large range of industries), this means that the market tends to be less volatile when the economy goes through bad times. If the local market has only one or two industries (meaning, it is driven only by one or a couple of industries), this might have a bigger negative impact on the market, especially when it comes to its recovery. This means that employment might decrease quite a bit and take longer to pick up.

As I've mentioned, understanding the housing market is important when you're looking to invest in a certain area. Besides looking at local zoning laws to understand any regulations or restrictions that might have an impact on the market, you should also be looking at market trends. These trends include changes in the value of the properties as well as sales volumes. This information is important because it gives you a clearer picture of how the market might be changing and how healthy the market is, as well as the demand for certain types of properties.

Market conditions essentially determine if you're in a buyer's market or a seller's market. As I've mentioned before, a buyer's market is when there's more supply than demand or there are more people looking to sell than to buy, which makes the value of properties decrease. A seller's market is exactly the opposite and happens when there's more demand than supply, which means the value of the properties increases.

But you should also look at the median price trends, which are a middle point between high and low and a great indicator of current market activity. If the median price shifts, this often means there has been movement in the market. For instance, if the median price increases, this often means the local market is increasing, which favors the sellers (and so the value of properties increases). If the median price decreases, this means there are fewer sales on properties, and the market might be shifting against sellers. However, an increase in the median price could have other meanings. For instance, it could mean that the properties in the lower part of the market are selling, but it doesn't necessarily mean that the properties that cost more are selling. It's important that you have a clear understanding of the different divisions between the higher-priced and lower-priced homes in the local market.

You might also come across something called the market inventory, and it's crucial that you look at its trends. Essentially, inventory in this context means the number of properties for sale. In other words, it tells you how much supply is available in the market. Seasons can have a big effect on the rise and fall of market inventory. For instance, it is known that during spring, the real estate market picks up during that time of year. The opposite is true for winter and fall, as real estate tends to slow down. If you take the seasonality of it from the equation, you'll get a better idea of the inventory in that specific local market.

Another important metric to look at is the average days on the market (DOM), which tells you, on average, how long properties stay on the market before they sell or how long it takes to sell a property in that market. This will tell you how long it might take for you to sell your property, as well as the demand for properties in the area.

HOW CAN YOU GATHER MARKET DATA?

To fully assess the market's conditions, it is essential to obtain data from a number of sources. Real estate websites, particularly online platforms such as Realtor.com and Zillow, should be the first resource to check. These platforms make publicly accessible data available and provide full access to local market statistics such as sales prices and rental rates. Additionally, contacting local real estate agents for a report is a good step because their information is frequently more accurate than what internet platforms have.

Moreover, if you have a relationship with a local realtor, they may have access to much more relevant data than what is available online. In particular, they can provide useful information about current market circumstances.

There's also broader data that you can gather from the government or economic data that might give you a hint of what the overall market looks like. You can go directly to government sources or the chambers of commerce to get that data.

Based on all the data you've collected and the assessment you've made, you should be better prepared to adapt your strategy to the current market. For instance, if the market assessment tells you that properties are appreciating quickly, you might want to adopt a long-term buy-and-hold strategy. But a market assessment is not something that you do only before you are about to make an investment decision; this is something that should be ongoing. It's important not only because it can help you mitigate any risks, but also because it allows you to anticipate any opportunities in the future.

MAKING DECISIONS BASED ON THE DATA GATHERED

Most of the decisions you will make in the real estate industry have to come from the data you collect. As we've seen, the real estate market is influenced by many different factors, and going through and understanding them requires great analysis, not just intuition. In this section, I will be talking about why data-driven decisions are important. Without them, it gets very hard to become successful in this business.

As I've stated before, decisions based on data gathered and analyzed allow you to mitigate the risks of every investment. When you properly analyze trends, economic indicators, and so on, you can make much better decisions, which automatically reduces some of the risks of the investments you make. Data is objective and unbiased, so it tells you what might work and what won't, regardless of your preferences. For instance, you might really like a property you've found, but if the data tells you that it's not a good investment, you should drop it and find something that better aligns with your financial goals. Data also allows you to understand if an investment is aligned with your goals and how much you can expect in returns when you invest in the property.

While you might have a good understanding of the market cycles, nothing is more accurate than data when it comes to really understanding what cycle the market is in or even what type of market is taking place. Data helps you choose the best possible investment strategy and mitigate risks. It can also lead to optimized returns on your investments because it allows you to identify investments that might give you better income potential or have a better appreciation over time.

When you're making data-driven decisions, you have to consider different aspects. Some of these we've already covered, such as market research, property analysis, economic indicators, or comps, but there are other things to consider as well. For example, market sentiment is relevant. Here, you need to understand if there's a positive sentiment toward the market or a negative one. This feeling has to do with the confidence of real estate investors in general. It can also be a driver of investment activity, which often leads to the appreciation of property.

The tools and overall technology used to gather this market data are important, too. For example, it is a good idea to search for data sources and systems that provide real-time information, as more recent and exact data is preferable. Also, though they develop financial estimations, these projections are founded on the gathered data. They provide a framework for making better-educated decisions about possible earnings, financing, and costs, among other things.

Let's have a look at the different tools and other resources you can use to gather important market data. I've mentioned some of these platforms and tools before, such as Zillow, that have great databases, market statistics, and historical data that you can peruse and that will help you gather essential information. When collecting all of this data, I find it useful to add it to a spreadsheet, such as Excel or Google Sheets. What's important is that you have all that data organized and can have a clear overview of the data gathered so you can examine it when needed. There is also dedicated professional real estate analytics software such as SmartZip, TopHap, or TopProducer, all of which feature more advanced tools to help you analyze data with predictive modeling.

Regardless of your choice, market research is continuous work that you have to do, and you have to remain committed to it throughout your career. As you perform these tasks, you will get more experienced with them and develop more skills, which will make this work easier. While data is important, when analyzing it, your knowledge and experience are as well, so don't only rely on data to make your decisions. Take into account your skills and knowledge so you can better mitigate potential risks.

However, it is true that most real estate investors heavily rely on data to make their decisions. This is because this approach has proven to be quite successful in the past, and as technology evolves, the insights we get from this data become more accurate, and so do your decisions. These two components, data and knowledge, are intrinsically connected, and they will help you make better choices during your career.

KNOWING WHEN TO ACT

Knowing when to act in real estate investing is part of having a successful business. It's an important moment when you decide to commit to an investment and take action after you've carefully analyzed all the points we've discussed above. Timing is a vital factor that can have a significant impact on the success of your investment as well as its profitability. But why is timing so important?

Let's begin with timing and market conditions. These are critical considerations, whether you are currently going through a seller's or a buyer's market. Timing has a large impact on your ability to negotiate the price of properties. Often, investors prefer to wait for more favorable conditions before acting on their investments. However, choosing the best time goes beyond the initial investment and often refers to withdrawing from an investment. As you know, before you get into any investment, you have to have an exit plan, and timing is very important. This is because selling at the right moment can significantly increase your profits. This, coupled with market cycles, can play an important role in understanding when exiting a deal might be more profitable.

Knowing when to act comes down to all the factors I've mentioned above, such as market and property analysis, financial preparedness, local economic factors, market sentiment, comps, and even property inspection.

Something else you need to account for is your risk tolerance regarding your investment goals. For instance, if you don't like to take many or high risks, you probably have a more risk-averse profile, which means that you prefer stable goals and long-term returns. In this case, a buy-and-hold strategy might be more appropriate for your style. But if you think that timing is important and the faster you get profits, the better, then perhaps a fix-and-flip would be more suited to your investment style, though at the same time, the risks would increase.

Once you take into account all of these factors, you have to make a decision and put it into action. Timing is relevant once again, but timing doesn't always mean looking for the perfect moment where all conditions align (I mean, ideally, sure, but if you're always waiting for all the right parameters to align, you will never get anything done). You can act once you have the necessary data to make a decision and understand when you should shift your strategies. This is when experience comes in, and it's not all about data and numbers (although these are important). Again, timing is important when you enter *or* exit a strategy, so keep that in mind when you're about to put your strategies into action.

Knowing the ways you can analyze deals and reach accurate numbers through due diligence is an important part of a real estate investor's life. Due diligence is a thorough process, and you shouldn't rush through it. You need to understand the risks and rewards and ensure your goals are aligned with the strategy. At the same time, mitigating risks will lower the chances of losing money and increase your profits. As we've seen in this chapter, due diligence encompasses many different things, such as evaluating market conditions or inspecting properties. Every decision you make should be based on the data collected from your due diligence and the experience you gain along the way. Sure, timing also plays an important role, but this aspect will become clearer as you understand how the industry works.

PROPERTY VALUATION

Knowing how to value a property can help you with analyzing your deals and later on when negotiating. While you should always get a survey or appraisal and look into comparable properties in the market or those that have recently sold, there are other ways you can consider a property's value. In fact, looking at comps while doing your own valuation is the best way to get a more accurate valuation of the property.

There are five main methods that you can use: the comparable method, the investment method, the profit method, the residual method, and the depreciated replacement cost method.

COMPARABLE METHOD

The comparable method is perhaps the easiest one. You can do it by looking at comparable properties that recently sold in the local area.

If we look at two identical properties in the same market, one sold for $130,000 and the other for $100,000, there are two things that we can conclude. First, the buyer of the $130,000 overpaid because they didn't gather enough information or pay for a building survey to analyze the extent of the work needed. On the other hand, the buyer of the $100,000 underpaid, probably because the seller didn't market the property correctly and didn't do their research. So, it's vital that, when buying or selling, you look at comps.

As a rule of thumb, when valuing a property, the last 20% of the value is often subjective. The thing is, there are no clear rules when it comes to valuing a property, and everything is based on speculation. For instance, if you were to ask five different surveyors about one property, they would probably give you five different prices for the property. It all comes down to how much the buyer is willing to pay, and that's why you should also look at intrinsic value.

You might have heard of intrinsic value, or perhaps not, but it essentially means the value the property has to the potential buyer. While comparable sales prices help narrow down the value of a property, it is the intrinsic value given by the buyer that ultimately matters. Sometimes, we come across a property that surprises us by selling for such a high price; that's probably because it meant something to the buyer.

Often, the reason to pay an extra $20,000 or $30,000 has nothing to do with money, but with the buyer's preference. For instance, if, by buying that particular property, the buyer doesn't have to commute to work or the kids can walk to school instead of taking the bus, it might make a massive difference to them. Therefore, they will be willing to pay the extra to outbid any other competition.

While comparing properties is merely a guide, it's still important to understand how you do it. Say that you're looking at a property where the house next to it was recently sold. If that house is 20% bigger than the one you're looking at and the bathroom has been refurbished, it's only natural that the property you're looking at costs less. If there are repairs to be made that will cost, say, $30,000, you can also reduce the offer.

When you're purchasing your first investment property, it's quite common that you go for the asking price, not knowing that this price is often already inflated (at least 10% to 15%) so buyers can negotiate. This means that if you make an offer for the asking price, you are probably offering a little too much (not counting intrinsic value). Here, the best way to know this is by looking at the local property market trends and seeing if the prices are going up or down.

INVESTMENT METHOD

This method is specially crafted for investors, and it determines the amount of money you would pay for a property based on certain metrics. When using this method, you are comparing the prices of properties to anticipate the rate of return. When you find the rate of return, then you can better measure the estimated price you want to pay.

When it comes to determining the investment value, you have to go through some steps. The first is to do comparable sales, as we did in the last method. Here, all you have to do is compare the value of comparable properties in the same area. Then, you have to look at the gross rent multiplier (GRM), where you measure the value of the investment by multiplying the gross rent you're projecting the property will make in a year by the GRM. You also need to know the cash-on-cash return, and you can calculate this number by dividing the first year's pro forma cash (which is a projected cash flow statement) by the total initial investment.

Then, you have to calculate the direct capitalization, where you convert an estimate of the first year's income into value to determine the market value of the property. Let's get into more detail.

As I've mentioned, analyzing some of the metrics will help you make better decisions, especially when calculating cash flow and rate of return to understand how profitable the investment might be. But what exactly is the capitalization rate (or cap rate)? Essentially, this is the needed rate of return on your investment, depreciation, or net value appreciation. In other words, the cap rate helps you estimate the resale value of the investment when it's time to sell. You can then apply this rate of the net operating income (NOI) to find the present value of your investment.

So, say that you expect to get a NOI of $500,000 over the next five years. If you discount the cap rate of 10% , the current market value of the property would be $5 million since market value = net operating income/cap rate. If you buy the property for $4 million, that would be a good deal, but if you bought it for more than $5 million, you would have overpaid for it. (Of course, you can use any numbers corresponding to the reality of your situation.)

Coming up with the cap rate can be a great metric to start with when valuing a property investment. While there are different ways to calculate the cap rate, one of the easiest ways to do it is through the market-extraction method. Here, you have to find already available NOI and sale price data on comps. For example, if you want to purchase a property where you expect to generate $300,000 in NOI and you have found three comps, Property 1 has a NOI of $150,000 and a sale price of $1.5 million, so the cap rate is 10% . The second property has a NOI of $200,000 and a sale price of $2.5 million, so the cap rate is 8% . Lastly, the third property has a NOI of $100,000 and a sale price of $2 million, so the cap rate is 5% . Then, you have to find the cap rate average by adding all the cap rates of the comps and dividing it by three (in this particular case), which is 7.6% , which is a good representation of the current market. Now that you have found the cap rate, you can better determine the market value of the property you want to invest in.

In this investment method, to find the valuation of a property, you can go a little further and look at two sub-categories of valuation methods: absolute and relative. The absolute valuation tells you the current value of potential incoming cash flows to find the intrinsic value of the property. Here, the most common methods are the discounted cash flow (DCF) and the dividend discount model (DDM), but I'm not going to dwell on them, as these are quite advanced techniques. But then there's the gross income multiplier (GIM), which belongs to the relative valuation, which is far easier to use.

With the GIM, you have to assume that properties in the same location are proportionally valued to the gross income they generate. For instance, let's say that you want to buy a 50,000-square-foot property, and by looking at comps, you find out that the average gross income per month per square foot in that area is $10. From here, you can assume that the gross annual income is $6 million since $10 x 12 x 50,000, but you need to account for vacant units during that time (assuming you rent out separate rooms or units). If you find out that the vacancy rate in that area is 6% , then the gross annual income will drop. Then, you would have to find the GIM and multiply it by the gross annual income, which you can look up online, such as in the area's chamber of commerce.

PROFITS METHOD

The profit method is more for commercial property, but you might use it in the future, so I'm just going to give you the basics. The main point here is the profitability of the tenants—in this case, the companies that occupy the property. Here, too, you can use the comparable method, but you would be looking at other businesses' profitability. For you to be able to use the profits method, there has to be a profitable business running on the property already, such as a cinema, a bar, or a hotel.

The first thing to do is to understand the key financials of the businesses for at least the last three or four years. Here, there are two main calculations you want to use: the gross profit and the net profit.

Gross profit = gross earnings - purchases

Net profit = gross profit - working expenses

Essentially, the gross earnings are the total revenue the business generates throughout the year, and the gross profit is the number after taking away the business purchase costs from the gross earnings.

In this context, working expenses are those that occur on a daily basis for the business, such as gas, water, business rates, and so on. The net profit is the gross earnings minus all the expenses. But how do you calculate rent?

Of course, you need to calculate the rent so you can properly evaluate the investment. Here, you could divide the net profit by half to determine a more accurate number. For example, say the gross earnings of the business currently on the property you are interested in purchasing are $500,000. The business purchases are

$200,000, and the business expenses are $150,000. Your calculations would go like this:

Gross profit = $500,000 - $200,000 = $300,000

Net profit = $300,000 - $150,000 = $150,000

Annual rent = 50% of $150,000 (net profit) = $75,000

RESIDUAL METHOD

This method is often used by investors who want to invest in land to determine its value. As always, you can also use the comparable method, but by using the residual method, you would be taking the developed value out of the land and subtracting the cost of developing it. Essentially, this method allows you to determine the value remaining after all the costs of developing the land are subtracted.

This is also a great way to estimate the costs, returns, and profits of land that you want to develop, as well as determine the budget needed and mitigate the risk of the development project. In other words, it allows you to find out if the land is worth buying and developing.

The calculations would look something like this:

Residual value = gross development value (GDV) - total development costs (including profit)

Let's break this down. GDV is essentially the market value of the project when developed, where you have to factor in the likelihood of renting the property after it is built. The profit is the value you might be willing to accept. Then, you have to consider the total development costs, which are the cost of the land plus any taxes you need to pay. Then there are the actual construction costs, which are likely to be estimated. There are also fees because you have to add in professional fees outside the building costs, such as environmental impact assessment, legal fees, or planning consultant fees.

You must also consider sales costs, which are usually the agent's fees and any commission you've agreed on; the cost of financing, which includes interest on borrowed money; and contingency costs.

DEPRECIATED REPLACEMENT COST METHOD

This type of valuation method is often used in properties that are highly specialized (as in custom-built) and would be hard to replace if lost. The depreciated replacement cost (DRC) can help you value an asset and take into account its depreciation over time, as well as the cost of replacing the asset if it is lost. This means that it is more applicable to commercial properties, such as labs or custom-made warehouses.

You can calculate the DRC by estimating the cost to replace the property, which can be done by assessing any changes in the cost of materials, as well as specialized labor when this property was initially built or purchased, and by subtracting the depreciation that happened over time.

For example, if you have a commercial property and want to know its value, you first look at how much it cost when it was first built —say, $2 million 15 years ago. The building has an estimated useful life of 40 years, as well as an annual depreciation rate of 3%. So, you would have:

$2 million - ($2 million x 3% x 15) = $1.1 million

If we assume that the cost of building something similar would be $1.5 million, and we want to know the DRC of the building, then:

DRC = current value + replacement cost - depreciation

DRC = $1.1 million + $1.5 million - ($1.5 million x 3% x 15), or DRC = $1.1 million + $1.5 million - $675,000 = $1,925,000

Thus, the DRC of the building is $1.92 million.

The emphasis of this chapter was on how you can analyze your deals. We first looked at how important due diligence is when it comes to making informed decisions. This is especially true if you want to protect your interests, which you definitely should.

Then, I broke down the different components of due diligence:

- Property inspection, where you hire a professional inspector to check the property.
- Financial analysis, where you need to dig into the finances of the property, such as rental demand, ROI, NOI, and other metrics to try and find out if the property is a good investment.
- Title search, where you verify the ownership of the property and check if there are any outstanding legal disputes.
- Market analysis, where you research the local market conditions, trends, and so on.
- Assessment of any legal and regulatory compliance to which you must adhere.

Remember that there is a time constraint when performing your due diligence, which you can find in the purchase agreement.

When evaluating the property, the inspector will then give you a detailed report about the structural integrity of the property and any other issues you will have to solve, which you can then add as contingencies in the purchase agreement to protect yourself.

You also have to research the current market conditions, where you have to consider different economic factors, such as property supply and demand, among others. This is also when you try to figure out the real estate cycle you are currently in to determine if it's a buyer's or a seller's market.

Gathering market data is also an important thing to do when analyzing your potential deals. You can use different websites, talk to real estate agents, or look at economic data online. But this is not something that you do only once; this type of data changes over time, so you have to be aware of any changes and be able to adapt your strategy accordingly.

With this data, you can then make better decisions to mitigate some of the risks associated with these types of investments. However, knowing when to act is just as important. While you shouldn't be waiting for the perfect time when everything perfectly aligns (which might never happen), you can't jump into an investment at any time. You have to consider certain factors, such as your finances, your risk tolerance, or your goals. Keep in mind that at the beginning, the right time will never seem to come, but as you get more experienced, it will become clearer to you.

Remember to continue to learn so you can continue to adapt your strategy as the market changes and as you gain more knowledge and experience. You will never know everything, but it's crucial that you never stop learning.

FREE GIFT #4

The Ultimate Due Diligence Checklist: Don't let anything slip through the cracks!

This essential tool will guide you through every step of your property evaluation and help you make well-informed decisions in your investment choices.

To get instant access this free e-book, scan the QR code below or visit this link: www.readstreetpress.com/realestatebonus4

8

STEP FIVE – MAKE AN OFFER THEY CAN'T REFUSE

Don't wait to buy real estate, buy real estate and wait.

– T. Harv Eker

The first offer might be a little intimidating for a real estate investor. It seems like such a complicated step and overly overwhelming at times, but it doesn't have to be that way.

In this chapter, we will be going through the whole purchasing process so you can have a better idea of the different steps you have to take to make your first offer. We will go through things like how you can create a compelling offer, how you can negotiate effectively, and even how you can handle inspections and contingencies. Making an offer is the sixth step to entering the real estate industry.

OVERVIEW OF THE PURCHASING PROCESS

When looking at the purchasing process, the first thing you have to do is define your investment goals. These goals will guide you through the whole purchase process and help you stay focused on what you want. After that, you have to come up with a budget that determines what you can and can't afford. This budget should factor in expenses such as renovations, closing costs, and a myriad of other ones.

As we've talked about, you have to get prequalified and preapproved. Doing so will allow you to increase your chances of getting the financing you need, as well as estimate the investment you can actually afford.

Once all of that is done, you have to find the property you want to invest in. Here, as you might know, you have to do your due diligence and evaluate the property, and only then can you think about making an offer. When making this offer, you have to add a few things, like the purchase price, any contingencies you might want to add, and a proposed timeline to perform all the contingencies.

This all seems a little overwhelming, right? But at this point, you should have an expert who will guide you through it and help you draft the proposal.

Once you've sent your proposal, chances are that negotiation is imminent, but I'll go through this particular step later on, where we will also talk about counteroffers, discussions of terms, and anything else related to the proposal. For now, you should only focus on doing your due diligence, as it will help you through the whole process.

If you have enough money to make such a purchase, then it's best to work closely with the lender to make sure everything goes according to plan. You are at the stage where you have to have an appraisal done, figure out the approximate value of the property, and ensure all the requirements are met by the lender. Then there's the contingency period, or a certain time period when you can ask the lender to repair some of the things; if not, you can withdraw from the deal if you don't reach an agreement. At the same time, you must have property insurance to ensure that you are protected against any damage or loss to the property.

Then, of course, there's the closing of the deal, which is the last step of the purchasing process. At this point, you will have to sign any remaining documents and transfer the funds.

CRAFTING A COMPELLING OFFER

This might not seem like a crucial step, but it is. Many real estate investors overlook the crafting of a compelling offer, though it can place you in a much more advantageous position. Essentially, you have to really show the seller how interested you are in purchasing the property. And by crafting a compelling offer, you can stand out from the crowd.

Of course, you need to know a few things, such as understanding the current market. To do this, you need to do your market research. Specifically, you need to be aware of current market conditions, the value of local properties similar to the ones you want to invest in, and so on, so you can create a stronger offer. Working with a realtor at this stage is quite important, given they have a great knowledge of the local market. But time is of the essence at this point, and you have to move fast, as there may be others interested in the property.

After all of that comes the offer price. When calculating your price, keep in mind that your offer has to be competitive, and you can determine this amount by looking at the average local market value. Again, this value is established through comps and your research. While lowballing might be tempting, try to send a fair offer, even if it is a little lower, so you can negotiate. Sending a very low offer decreases the chances of not having your offer accepted and the seller picking someone else's. At this point, you have to be ready to negotiate and always leave some room in your budget so you can increase the price during the negotiations if needed.

At this point, you have to add the earnest money deposit when sending your offer so that you show the seller you are a committed buyer. If everything goes as planned, your offer will appeal to them.

Let's move on to contingencies now. These are important clauses that allow you to protect yourself and your interests. These can be anything, but there are a few that are more common than others, such as appraisal, financing, or property inspection. It's important that you are as specific as possible when writing about these contingencies, especially about the conditions of meeting them.

The finance preapproval, which is commonly represented by the preapproval letter I previously mentioned, comes next in the process. This letter, which established your position as a well-qualified buyer, should be included with your offer. Consider including a personal letter to the seller, emphasizing your serious wish to purchase the property and explaining your vision for its use. When setting a closing date, it's best to provide some wiggle room to accommodate the seller's needs.

You also need to take into account escalation clauses. These clauses allow you to increase the bid price for the property if it is matched by another potential buyer. This not only proves your commitment to buying the property, but also ensures that you are always above the highest bidder (of course, there should be amount restrictions).

Also, make sure you send your offer in a timely manner and maintain your professionalism at all times throughout the negotiation process. Having a positive attitude can go a long way with the seller.

To be honest, crafting an offer to invest in a property is as much an art as it is experience and knowledge of the local market. This offer is you trying to convince the seller that you are the best buyer with the best offer, and you really have to focus on it if you want to increase your chances of success.

NEGOTIATING EFFECTIVELY

Negotiation is a big step in the offer process for your potential property. Even when you eventually sell the property, it's important to have strong negotiation skills so you can maximize your profits. Now, as I've said multiple times, understanding the market is key, as is setting clear goals as to how much you want to purchase or sell. Bringing in an experienced realtor is also vital, as they can provide great insights throughout the process.

Now that we have that out of the way, building rapport with the seller (or buyer) is also one of the most important aspects. You need to be able to foster trust, maintain professionalism, and have open communication with them. During this phase, the more prepared you are, the better. Gather all the information you might need, and most important of all, know your limits. You have to determine your budget beforehand, or the price you are willing to accept if you are a seller. Understanding the other party's motivation can give you insights into their goals and give you more chances to tailor your negotiation strategy better, or even come up with solutions that might suit both of you.

I can't emphasize enough how important effective communication is at this stage. You not only have to maintain professionalism, but you also have to actively listen to the seller because you can figure things out without them even telling you; you can find common ground just by listening.

Now, onto the negotiation tactics. Ideally, you would want to go for a win-win approach where the outcome of the negotiations is favorable to both parties. Finding common ground is key here. However, this can't always be the case, but nevertheless, it should be something you strive to reach. Again, counteroffers are pretty common during negotiations, so be prepared for them. Consider every counteroffer that comes your way, and don't let emotions make the decisions. One last thing: You should be able to leverage the information you've gathered to help you with your arguments.

Above all, negotiations are a game of patience, and you should avoid rushing at all times. I'm going to be honest with you: most negotiations take time, and this is especially true if there are more than two parties involved. But trying to rush the process is not going to help you. Also, one thing that I always like to consider is introducing nonmonetary terms. This could be contingencies, closing dates (where you should always be flexible), or items such as appliances or repairs, for instance.

One last thing I think is very important throughout any negotiation is to have what in the real estate business is called a "walk-away point." This is the point where you need to know when to walk away from the negotiations if terms don't align or if the negotiations become irrational. If you continue after this point, you will just be losing time and potentially money.

So, when negotiating, there's a mix of knowledge, great communication skills, preparation, and patience. Above all, stay calm and don't rush the negotiation process because the more level-headed you are, the better the outcome will be.

When negotiating, it is important that you are aware of the type of market you're in: buyer's or seller's market. In a seller's market, as you know, the seller has the advantage in the negotiations, which means that if you're a buyer, you simply don't have as many options, and the sellers can further increase the prices on their properties.

For example, say you're a seller in a seller's market, and you place one of your investment properties on the market. On the first day, you have 20 showings, and on the second day, you have 15. In a buyer's market, having 35 showings in a month or two would be lucky, but in a seller's market, it's not. You receive five offers from these showings, and in two of these, the buyers would pay the difference (up to a certain amount) if the property appraised for less than the asking price. For example, if the property was on the market for $250,000, but the appraisal came only at $230,000, these two buyers would be happy to pay the $20,000 difference to close the deal quickly. This is just to say that in a seller's market, buyers are a little more desperate to buy a property, so they typically won't mind overpaying for a property.

In a buyer's market, the negotiations tilt toward the buyer. As you know, there's quite a lot of supply in terms of properties in this type of market, which means buyers have options. Because of this, the value of properties decreases.

If you're buying, then you can negotiate a few things. For instance, if a property is listed at $200,000 and has been on the market for four months without any good offers, you can argue that the current price exceeds the market, and you can try to bring it down. Because sellers are desperate to sell, they are more likely to take the chance to sell instead of continuing to pay costs, such as holding costs for a property they are not making any money on. You can also ask the seller to cover the closing costs, especially if they are not willing to reduce the price of the property.

Even when it comes to inspections, buyers have the upper hand. This is because most contracts have an inspection clause, which means that if the inspection reveals a big issue, the buyer can leave the deal or ask the seller to repair those issues. If this were in a seller's market, the seller might simply move on to another proposal.

TIPS FOR BUYERS AND SELLERS

One of the best tips I can give you as a buyer is to try to understand the needs of the seller. Many of the sellers will want to maximize their profits, of course, but sometimes, their goals might not have anything to do with money. This is where you need to try to come up with a solution. And so, you need to uncover the main reason that is driving the seller and how you can solve that problem for them. In other words, you need to understand their needs so you can negotiate effectively.

A couple of years ago, I found an off-market seller. In trying to understand his needs, I found out that he was moving into an assisted living facility and didn't have the money to pay for it. However, the house required a number of repairs. I figured out the needs of the seller by talking to him: he had to sell to get money to pay to move into the assisted living facility, and he needed the money fast. In my mind, besides getting the money quickly, the deal had to be convenient, and this is what motivated the seller even more than trying to maximize his profits. What I did was buy the property as quickly as I could (while still doing my due diligence), but I didn't require them to do any repairs, which was exactly what he needed. On the other hand, I got the property for a cheaper price.

As a seller, you need to figure out who your ideal buyer is. You should do this even before you put the property on the market. When you know exactly who your ideal buyer is, things become a lot easier, especially when it comes to marketing the property. You can look at it from two main categories, especially when you're negotiating a single-family home: those who are looking for their primary home, and investors looking for a distressed property.

The primary home buyer wants to find a house they can start living in right away, which means the property should be ready to be occupied and shouldn't need a ton of repairs. If you're selling a property to first-time buyers, you should have a home that is ready for them. This often means you need to envision yourself living there, so every repair or refurbishment you do has to cater to first-time buyers. Another thing to keep in mind is that chances are that these buyers will use financing to purchase the property, usually through traditional financing (which is, let's say, a 30-year mortgage), so the property has to meet some quality conditions for the lender.

If you are catering to real estate investors, then it is likely that these types of buyers use alternative types of financing, such as hard-money loans, cash, or any other type of creative financing. For you, the seller, the conditions of the property are not as relevant, as these types of buyers put more emphasis on the cost of the property, contingencies, and the closing timeline, for example. It is also likely that such buyers will use a fix-and-flip strategy, so it's important that you understand this process because they might have a predetermined budget and, during negotiations, they will try to lower the price. What happens quite often is that these buyers will bring an inflated renovation budget to try to lower the cost of the property. In these cases, you might want to perform an inspection so you can counter-offer their initial proposal.

Let's look at tips regarding off-market properties, given these types of negotiations might be a little different. The main difference here is the needs of the seller. Usually, sellers with off-market properties have equity in the properties. For that reason, they have a certain motivation to sell the property, but cannot list their properties on the Multiple Listing Service (MLS) or on the market because the property is in need of major repairs.

I'll tell you a little secret: many sellers don't have enough skills to sell their properties. Meaning, they don't fully understand the buying and selling process of properties, which means that for you, this can be a great opportunity to negotiate. This is particularly true if the property they are selling is an inheritance (often because a parent or a family member passed away) and they were given the property but have not planned for such circumstances. Moreover, these sellers often have other things to care about. This doesn't mean you should take advantage of such a situation, but from a buyer's standpoint, you can still make a good deal without ripping them off. Instead, you can act as the expert and help solve their problems while making a good deal. Often, these sellers will not bring a lawyer because they think they will just sell the property quickly, in which case you can bring a real estate attorney to make their lives easier and make the process smoother (here, you will also be paying for the services of the attorney as part of the contract and to decrease the property's cost). This is a win-win situation because the sellers don't have to go through the estate process by themselves, and you make a good deal for yourself.

When you prioritize the seller's needs, building a relationship with them will make it easier to find common ground. For instance, if you first contact the seller, you will ask them what their needs are. The truth is, you might not get to their true need right away, but you've started working on the relationship. Then, it is likely that you will meet face to face and see the property, and here, your chances of building that relationship increase if you look for common ground. You should also try to connect on a personal level. For instance, if there's any reference to their hobbies, such as playing the guitar or a poster of a sports team, you can start breaking the ice with that. Essentially, you need to find a way to bond. Make sure that this bond is truthful; don't come up with lies or any other type of disingenuous behavior. Eventually, you will find common ground. Any common interests you might have are the foundation of the relationship you want to build, so they have to be sincere.

While going to a property for the first time, you should pay attention to the details as much as possible. You can ask a few questions, such as, "When was the boiler last replaced?" "When were the drywall repairs?" and many other things. The main goal here is to try to find out as much as you can so you can use this as leverage when negotiating to lower the property's cost. The seller might also ask you questions, and a prominent one is how much you want to pay for the property. You should always try to deflect the question.

When you're on the lookout for a property (especially when these are potential sellers who have yet to make up their minds about selling), you can ask to be either the first-in buyer or the last-in buyer. The first-in buyer means you are the first buyer to make an offer, and the last-in buyer means you are requesting to be the last one to make an offer. There are advantages and disadvantages to both of these options.

If you are the first buyer to make a proposal, you have the advantage of being the first, which increases the chances that a seller will accept your offer, especially if they are motivated to sell. However, while the seller might be motivated, this doesn't mean they will accept your proposal right away, and they might want to wait for other offers before they commit to one. If you are the last-in buyer, you will know all the previous offers, which is an advantage so you can alter your offer as needed. However, while you wait (as the last-in buyer), the seller might have already accepted another offer. For that reason, many investors prefer to be the first-in, especially if the seller is motivated to sell and will jump at the first opportunity to sell the property.

Let's now consider negotiating tips on MLS properties, which are dedicated more to sellers. When selling with MLS, using an agent is important, especially if you have renovated the property. Essentially, listing the property with the MLS exposes your property to more potential buyers, whether they are homeowners or investors. Also, if your property is listed in the MLS, it means that agents can access your listing from anywhere, which means that primary buyers and investors wanting to purchase a property in your area will also see it, giving you more leverage when it comes to potential buyers, as you don't have to rush into the first offer. Here, when you're listing on the MLS, the two more important parameters for buyers are: the condition of the property, and the price.

To give you an idea of an agent's importance when selling a property, they can bring knowledge of the market and jump into negotiations with buyers, which is more than justification for the commission they receive. In fact, if you're selling the property after you've flipped it, you should add these costs to your budget from the beginning. The only exception to this would be if you're going through a great seller's market and know you will sell the property for a great price. Either way, if you list your property on the MLS, you are almost guaranteed a few shows, which is why you should have your agent do a follow-up on the potential buyers. Here, the agent can ask them what their general thoughts are of the property, or what they thought about the property's conditions. If nothing comes of it, at least you will know what potential buyers think of the property and start to see a pattern, even if it's negative. When this happens, you can simply wait and not change the price of the property until there's an offer from a buyer, but keep in mind that this might cost you while the holding costs continue to pile up. Or you can listen to the buyer's feedback and make the change so they can make an offer on the property.

Alternatively, you can always offer seller financing, especially if you are in a buyer's market. The truth is, regardless of the market, there are many potential buyers who might have a hard time qualifying for traditional financing. This could be because they don't have the money for a down payment or because they don't have a high enough credit score. So, for these types of buyers, seller financing might be the solution, and it might be a good way for you to get an offer on your property. But as we've learned, there are disadvantages to this, such as the fact that you need to be the lender. Many investors don't want to do this; however, if you're okay with it, then it might be a great solution for you.

Remember one thing: you can negotiate almost anything when dealing with transactions in real estate, regardless of whether you're buying or selling a property, but you should always try to get a win-win situation out of it. You should understand the needs of the other party first and foremost so you can gain leverage and negotiate a great deal.

DEALING WITH COUNTEROFFERS

You know that counteroffers are quite common during negotiations, and because of that, I'm dedicating a section to them. Many new real estate investors don't know how to deal with them in the first place.

The first thing I want to say is that you should always be expecting a counteroffer. If you do that, you can anticipate your response. When you submit your initial offer, always think about what counteroffer the other party might ask for. Always analyze the counteroffer even if, at first glance, it might look like a bad one. Take the time to review it and pay special attention to any specific terms and conditions, such as timelines, contingencies, or changes in price.

However, your objectives should be prioritized here, so when you make an initial offer and review a counteroffer, always refer to your goals and decide which terms might and might not be negotiable, as well as those areas where you might have a little more flexibility. Also, don't let the other party wait for too long. Timely communication is important and shows respect, and delayed responses might lead to frustration from the other party. Regardless of how bad or even ridiculous the counteroffer might be, always keep your emotions in check because, in the worst-case scenario, you can simply leave the negotiations.

Also, every time you get a counteroffer, you should check with your realtor for any guidance they might be able to give you. They have ample experience in this regard and can offer some help. Now, when you get a counteroffer, most people think you can do two things: you either follow with another counteroffer, or you accept it. But there are always three options: you can submit another counteroffer with revised terms, you can accept the counteroffer as proposed, or you can simply reject it if the terms of the counteroffer are nowhere near what you want.

Remember that, regardless of negotiations back and forth and the flexibility you might have, you have to stay within your budget. So, you have to make sure that any adjustments to the price align with your financial capabilities. Counteroffers are also great ways to gain a little bit more insight into the other party's motivations. Understanding their goals might help you counter their offer more efficiently.

Apart from consulting your realtor, you should also bring in a financial advisor as well as a legal advisor when you receive a counteroffer. This is to ensure that the terms of the counteroffer are legal and beneficial to you. Remember to set a walk-away point. This is the point when you don't believe you can reach a fair negotiation with the seller, so you simply walk away from the deal. This is important because it will allow you to just move on instead of wasting time on an investment that will not pan out or bring you any advantage.

When dealing with counteroffers, there are a few skills at work here. First, you need to be adaptable to any changing circumstances. Make sure your focus is on your goals, but be flexible in that you want to find a good solution for both parties. Rely on your advisors because they can give you great insights on how to navigate these counteroffers and still benefit you.

HANDLING CONTINGENCIES AND INSPECTIONS

Contingencies and inspections are key parts of the purchasing process. They both protect your interests and help with the implementation of the deal.

Contingencies describe any requirements that must be met before a negotiation can be formalized. Inspections, appraisals, or financial requirements are some of the most common contingencies added to the purchase agreement. As I've previously said, you should always bring an expert when amending the purchasing agreement to ensure that the phrasing of these contingencies is done properly and there are no loopholes that might lead to conflicts down the line.

For example, if you add a home inspection contingency, you are allowing yourself the chance to hire an inspector to make a report on the condition of the property. The main goal of hiring one is to find any issues with the property you are not aware of that might influence your investment. After their inspection, the expert will give you a detailed report of any issues they have found, such as necessary repairs or safety issues.

If there are any urgent repairs that need to be done, you can negotiate them with the seller. Usually, it goes one of two ways: the seller fixes them before you purchase the property, or you fix them, but the selling price of the property lowers so you can take on the cost of repairs. If you can't reach an agreement with the seller after a few counteroffers, you can abandon the deal.

Financing contingencies are often on the buyer's side. If you can't get financing within a certain period of time, the seller can withdraw from the negotiations without losing a single dollar. You might be asking, "But I have been preapproved; how can I not get financing?" A preapproval doesn't mean you have been approved yet; it's only a good indication that you will get approved and show the seller that you are a serious buyer.

Appraisal contingencies allow the buyer to order an appraisal to find a more accurate value of the property. For example, if the property you want to purchase comes out for less than the purchase price the seller established, you can ask the seller to decrease the price. If that request is denied, you can leave the negotiations. The appraisal, however, is usually ordered by the lender and done by a qualified appraiser, who does a detailed evaluation of the value of the property based on comps.

Most contingencies have deadlines, and it's key to adhere to them. Failure to do so may result in the sacrifice of some rights.

Navigating all of this can be a little overwhelming, but you have to really consider it, especially with a professional who can guide you through it. Remember that all of this is vital to protecting your interests and ensuring everything runs smoothly, from the negotiations to the transactions.

So, we've seen how to make an offer and go through the contingencies and counteroffers. Remember, creating a compelling offer needs careful consideration of the market conditions, as well as understanding your budget and your goals. You can really turn around negotiations with contingencies by protecting your finances.

Also, always expect counteroffers, and always try to be one step ahead of the other party. However, never forget your goals, and if negotiations are straying a little too far from your objectives, feel free to walk away.

KEY TAKEAWAYS

- Define your investment goals and know your budget so you can stay focused on them during negotiations.
- Prequalifications and preapprovals will give you leverage in negotiating terms and help you know what you can afford.
- Make a compelling offer with a competitive price based on the local market value.
- If you can, build rapport with the seller and find out their needs to reach a win-win situation and be ready for a counteroffer.
- Knowing the seller's motives can help you anticipate what they are going to counter with so you can respond effectively and quickly.
- Set a walk-away point when you think you won't get anywhere so you don't waste time.
- Build in financial contingencies to protect yourself if the deal doesn't go through. Have contingencies in the offer based on inspections as well.

9

STEP SIX – CLOSE YOUR FIRST DEAL & COLLECT THE KEYS TO YOUR KINGDOM

Find out where the people are going and buy the land before they get there.

— WILLIAM PENN ADAIR

Now that you know how to make an offer and how negotiations can go, it's time to understand how you can close a deal. You might think that all you have to do after the lengthy negotiations is sign the papers and it's all done, but it's never like that. This is the last step when it comes to acquiring an investment property.

THE CLOSING PROCESS

The closing process is the final step in the purchasing process. If successful, you will become the owner of the property, but this is not simply signing some papers; there's a bit more that goes into it. Let's go through the parts and first focus on what happens just before the closing process.

At this point, you have to conduct a title search to ensure the property is indeed under the ownership of the seller and that there are no outstanding disputes. Essentially, this will tell you if the seller does have the right to sell you the property. Also, at this point, it's important that you get another look at the property, especially if there exist any contingencies, such as repairs, to ensure that these are resolved.

After that is completed, you have to go through the closing disclosure. This is a document that outlines the final details of the transaction, such as the closing costs or the purchasing price. Only then can you start signing the documents. There are a few of them that you have to sign and can include promissory or mortgage notes, deeds, and so on, but your legal representative can help you understand all of this as you sign.

After everything is signed, the next step is the transfer of funds. Usually, this process can be separated into two distinct parts: funds for purchases and funds for closing costs. The first often happens when the buyer gives a cashier's check or has a wire transfer done. This is to cover the purchase of the property and the down payment. Essentially, this is the big chunk of the money. The funds for closing are always the responsibility of the buyer. These can include costs such as appraisals, legal services, and so on. Let's have a look at the most common costs.

The lender's fee is customary, which can include application fees, origination fees, and any other costs and charges regarding the mortgage. Title and escrow charges cover title searches, insurance, and escrow accounts. Recording fees are also standard, and involve the recording of the transfer of the property paid to the local government. Of course, if you've used a real estate agent, they will also take a fee or a commission, but this often falls on the seller's side.

At this stage, you should have a closing agent, an expert who will guide you in the transfer of funds, as well as with the ownership papers. This is often an attorney who knows about this particular aspect, but it can also be a title company. This is just so you know that the funds are allocated properly. Then there's the deed of transfer, which happens when the seller signs the documents and ownership is officially transferred to you. While this is happening, the local government is simultaneously recording ownership as well.

When that's all done, there are a few other things you have to finish. For instance, you need to establish a date of possession of the property, setting a date for the seller to hand the keys to you so you can finally have access to the property. The possession date is usually stipulated in the agreement, and while the handing of the keys and possession date can occur on the same day, it doesn't necessarily have to be that way. If that's the case, then the handing of the keys is always after the possession date.

You and your legal expert have to make sure that the closing process complies with both legal and regulatory requirements. You don't necessarily have to know the ins and outs of this procedure, but that's why you should have an expert with you. This is important because there might be some tax implications depending on the type of transaction or the jurisdiction in which you reside. At this point, bringing in a tax professional might ease the process and give you peace of mind.

While this all might sound a little complicated, with the help of experts, you shouldn't have to worry about it, and it can actually go pretty fast. Don't do this on your own, even if you think you have some expertise in the subject. It's always better to have a second or even third pair of eyes on these occasions, as you might stumble into some legal issues down the road that you could have easily avoided.

Once this is all done, you can finally become a property owner.

REQUIRED PAPERWORK AND DOCUMENTATION

You need to know, more or less, what you are signing. You don't have to know every detail of it, but at least have a general idea, even if you're working with a professional. There are typically many documents to sign, but they're mostly there to protect the interests of both parties.

I've mentioned the purchase agreement before, which is basically a document that outlines the terms and conditions of the proposed sale. These terms can include, but are not exclusive to, the purchase price, contingencies, or possession date. There are other papers that you need to sign as well. For example, there are inspections, deeds, appraisals, closing disclosures, or title insurance policies. There also tends to be a property survey, so you know with certainty that the property is legal under the seller's name.

If you are the buyer, then when it comes to the affidavit of title, you may relax because the seller is in charge of handling that. This document proves the seller's clear title and the absence of any claims. However, as the buyer, you must verify that you have all of the appropriate documentation related to the escrow account, including instructions and an agreement, in order for the monies to be distributed properly.

Don't forget to keep all loan paperwork, including the deed of trust or mortgage, the note, and any lender-specific documentation. In some areas, when specific property disclosures are required by law, the seller must make a seller disclosure. Both the buyer and the seller must provide proof of insurance coverage in the form of their separate insurance policies. Additionally, depending on your area, there may be numerous federal or state-mandated documents to guarantee compliance with regulatory and legal norms.

You see, there's a lot that you need to have or hand over. Navigating through these can be overwhelming, but this can all be accomplished with a competent real estate lawyer. They can also guide you through the whole process; it's what they do, after all. Still, it's vital that you comply with everything if you don't want the process to take longer than it should, or even go awry.

WORKING WITH TITLE COMPANIES AND ATTORNEYS

When going through these transactions in real estate, working with title companies and attorneys is quite common. They provide essential insights into making sure that the financial and legal aspects of the transaction are all properly handled. Let's go through their roles and how you can work with them.

Title companies can provide many services, such as title searches, where they verify the history of the property's ownership and make sure there are no claims or disputes. They also offer title insurance policies that serve to protect the lender and the buyer in case there are any issues down the road. They often also provide escrow services, or accounts where funds regarding the transaction are held, and make sure that all parties fulfill their obligations and get paid.

Now, you should always do your due diligence when working with these companies, as you would with any company that provides you with services. You might want to go for one that has vast experience in the field and a solid reputation. Communication in this phase with these companies is extremely important, especially during the closing process.

Real estate attorneys offer other things. They have extensive legal expertise in real estate and can offer you guidance throughout the whole process. They can also prepare documents for you and review them, such as deeds or purchase agreements. And if there are any disputes, they can chime in, provide guidance, and even negotiate on your behalf.

Choosing a real estate attorney is even more important than choosing a title company because the attorney's competence can differentiate a good deal from a bad one. Having experience is not the only thing you should be looking for; you should also have knowledge of the local market and be familiar with any regulations. These attorneys also offer legal consultation throughout the process and, as I've said, legal representation if you need it.

It's not uncommon for title companies and attorneys to work together to make the whole process smoother. They often share information and align their efforts to protect your interests. Because they have managed all the documents, they will collaboratively help you navigate all the paperwork that is necessary.

Working with these two entities is just part of the process, and when you first start, you will have to do your research to find good ones. But once you form a relationship with them and are happy with the results, you can continue to use them so you don't have to research every time you make a new investment.

Remember what I said about creating relationships? These are some that you want to establish as quickly as you can because they are always necessary.

POST-CLOSING RESPONSIBILITIES AND CONSIDERATIONS

After you've closed the deal, there are still things you need to do. If your plan is to rent out the property, then you have to get started with preparing the property for tenants. But before that, you have to record the deed with the county so the transfer is finally formalized.

One minor thing that many new real estate investors forget way too often is changing the locks once you become the owner of the property. You don't know who else, apart from the seller, has the keys to the property, so if you want to protect the property and future tenants, you must change the locks. You also have to update the insurance, despite becoming a landlord or just a homeowner. This is to ensure that you have the right insurance policy and don't run into any legal issues in the future. Remember to transfer the utilities or any other services that the previous owner might have on the property, such as water, gas, internet, and electricity. All of these now have to fall under your name, and you are responsible for them.

Be sure to do any repairs and maintenance needed before you bring in any tenants. You can have another look at the home inspection report to check for anything that the inspector might have flagged, and fix it. At this point, talking to a tax advisor might be important so you understand any taxes you might need to pay now that you are the owner.

If you're renting out the property, it's important that you address any concerns your tenants might have and that they are deemed reasonable. A happy tenant increases the chances of staying longer on the property, which might stabilize your cash flow and maximize your earnings. Keeping all the financial records is also important so you can understand how your investment is going and track the overall performance of the property, as well as when you start making a profit on it.

You still have responsibilities when you become the owner of the property. If anything, those responsibilities might increase, especially if you become a landlord.

Closing the deal is just as important as choosing the right investment for you or negotiating the deal. There are a few steps you have to go through and many documents to sign. You should ensure these are delivered in a timely manner and properly signed so the process goes smoothly and quickly. During this phase, preparation is everything, and when done properly, it can really pay off.

Get your team ready so they can help you navigate this process, which can take a little while. But with great professionals by your side, there's a higher chance that all of this will get wrapped up a lot faster.

KEY TAKEAWAYS

- Closing a deal is just as important as making an offer and negotiating. It's not over until it's over.
- Title searches are imperative to make sure the property has no outstanding disputes. Make sure final transactions are made (such as closing costs). Sign the documents (often many of them), transfer the funds, figure out the possession date, and check legal and regulatory compliance.
- Closing entails a ton of paperwork that needs to be signed, including the purchase agreement, insurance proof, loan paperwork, property surveys, deeds, appraisals, title insurance policies, and many others.
- Title companies conduct title search and often provide escrow services.

- Post-closing closing responsibilities include recording the deed to formalize the transfer of the property, updating the property insurance, updating utilities, or changing locks.
- Keep all financial records of the transfer in case you run into issues in the future. If you're going to rent, then you have the responsibility to screen tenants and ensure that their concerns are heard and addressed.

STEP SEVEN – EASILY MANAGE YOUR FIRST PROPERTY OR PROJECT & COLLECT YOUR FIRST CHECK

Buy real estate in areas where the path exists...and buy more real estate where there is no path, but you can create your own.

— DAVID WARONKER

Closing a deal is a great milestone that should be celebrated, but you have to start thinking about what your next steps should be, and it's vital that you have a plan. What I like to do after I close a property is review my goals, especially my long-term goals.

To start, ask yourself these questions: Do you want to acquire more properties? If yes, do you plan on diversifying your portfolio, or do you prefer to specialize in a certain niche? Either way, if you choose to continue to buy properties (and I'm not saying right away), you will be looking at ways to grow your portfolio. For that, you need to come up with a strategy to invest in more properties, going back to the various strategies we've talked about.

While you are recovering your money or accumulating more, it's important that you stay in the game. By this, I mean staying informed, checking property values in potential areas that you want to invest in, monitoring trends, and so on. You also have to continue to learn and hone your skills as much as you possibly can, whether it is looking up new strategies or acquiring more knowledge of real estate investing.

Let's take this opportunity to go over some of the things that I didn't talk about but that might be important.

MANAGING A FIX-AND-FLIP PROJECT

For any investment you make, you should always start with your due diligence, where you analyze the market, do a property inspection, and so on. You also have to create a budget and look at your financing options.

Now, what's different about fix-and-flip properties is that you need to plan your renovations carefully. You see, the more you budget and understand the things that increase the value of the property for a reduced cost, the more your profit goes up. So, renovation planning starts with devising a well-prepared scope of work where you highlight what renovations you have to do. Start with the essential renovations because these will allow you to pass inspection and sell the property; without them, the property will fail inspection, and you will not be able to sell it. In other words, these are needed. But also, outline all the other improvements and renovations that you think will increase the value of the property.

Then, if you don't have a contractor team, you best get one. Contractors are essential when it comes to fixing and flipping properties, and the more you work with the same company or team, the easier it will get for you—and the cheaper it will get. Then, you have to obtain all the necessary permits and comply with any regulations.

You also have to have project management skills, so creating a timeline for the renovations is important. You don't want to drag these things along because the more time passes, the more money you lose. During this phase, it's also crucial that you keep an eye on your expenses so they don't decrease your profit when you sell them.

When all is done, you have to market your property, which, as you know, comes with a cost, too. An efficient market will bring not just prospective buyers but the right potential buyers, saving you time filtering through buyers who will never buy your home. Then there's the cost of closing the deal and the time it takes to negotiate.

FINDING AND SCREENING TENANTS

This is a subject that we have yet to develop, but it's quite vital when you become a landlord. This doesn't necessarily mean just finding tenants; it's about finding the *right* tenants. Those who will take good care of your property, pay on time, and do everything a good tenant entails. If you don't find good tenants, chances are that you will find problems down the road, including reduced or delayed profits that might lead to eviction, a very time-consuming and lengthy process.

The first step when screening for great tenants is to market your property properly. There's a lot you can do when it comes to marketing your property, with many different strategies to choose from. Listing your property is important, and choosing the right platforms is, too. Platforms like Realtor.com or Zillow are great places to start. You shouldn't disregard social media platforms either, which are a great way to advertise your properties. You can also advertise them for free on these platforms.

Hiring a professional photographer to take quality pictures of your property can lead to great results and higher chances of your property being viewed. You can certainly do it yourself, but if you lack the expertise, I recommend hiring someone who is equipped. More often than not, the results come out much better. The presentation of the property is also important given this is what tenants will see. If you want to bring in quality tenants, these two things are important.

Then comes the tenant application process. While not necessary, I would have all potential tenants fill out a rental application so you have a better idea of who they are. Here, you should aim to collect personal details, employment information, rental history, and so on. Once that is done, you will analyze all the applications and screen them. This involves doing credit checks to assess for good credit history and a background check to understand if they have any prior convictions, verifying their income, and obtaining any references from previous landlords.

One thing that is quite important to know is the fair housing laws with which you have to comply. These laws are both federal and local, so make sure you understand them. They have to do with any discriminatory practices such as religion, gender, or race. I'm not saying that you'll break these laws on purpose, but if you don't understand them, you might be at risk when screening tenants.

Once you've chosen the right tenants, it's time for the lease agreement. These have to be clear and comprehensive, where you have to add the amount of rent, the date the rent is due, any security deposit, and all the responsibilities you have to fulfill, such as maintenance. Here, it's important that you go to your attorney before sending it out to tenants to sign, just to make sure that everything is done properly.

One last thing on tenants: communication is vital. I've said it many times in the most diverse stages of this whole process, but clear communication is the only way for you to know that everyone is on the same page. Make sure you decide the best way to contact your tenants, and they will contact you from the very beginning. If they have any concerns, make sure you address them promptly so you can build a great landlord-tenant relationship. You should also talk about the ground rules with your new tenants, and it's best that you do so in writing so they have it. These rules can encompass emergency procedures, property rules, and whom they should contact for any urgent repairs. Also, even with tenants on your property, you have to schedule inspections from time to time; it's just the law. So, when that happens, make sure to inform the tenants with a proper notice.

If you like your tenants and their lease is about to expire, you might want to consider offering them a lease renewal where you can discuss any changes to the lease or rent adjustments. However, you also have to be prepared for evictions if tenants violate the lease terms or don't pay rent. There's a whole legal procedure for that, and your attorney can help you with it.

PROPERTY MANAGING TIPS

The most common way to get into the real estate business is by buying a property and renting it to tenants, which means you are in it for the long haul. So, I think it's important to highlight some tips when it comes to managing the properties. Keep in mind that some of these I've already mentioned throughout the book, but it's important that you remember them.

Communication is vital, as I've said, so here, you want to respond to tenants as quickly as you can and provide them with emergency contacts if they have an urgent situation at hand. Preventive maintenance is something you want to do regularly, so you don't have to only do it when something happens and it costs you double to fix it. If you do this maintenance in a timely manner, your tenants will also appreciate it. Also, adopt some security measures to protect the property and the tenants, too; this could be anything from proper lighting to secure locks to security cameras.

Always be legally aware so you don't accidentally breach any law, such as fair housing laws or health and safety regulations. The same goes for your lease agreement; it should comply with the law, and you have to pass it on to your attorney before they send it out. Always keep proper records of all the documents having to do with the property, as this paperwork is the only way for you to accurately understand the property's profitability. This goes for the money coming in, but also any receipts or invoices.

To make things easier for you, think about digital solutions when it comes to rent collection so you don't have to waste time physically collecting rent. There are many different platforms that can help you streamline this process.

SCALING YOUR REAL ESTATE PORTFOLIO

When you start your business, even at the beginning, the aim is to scale your business, acquire more properties, and expand your portfolio. You can also expand your portfolio by simply increasing the value of your investments, which often happens naturally. However, to continue to scale your business, you first need to set some goals. Not only that, but you also have to set a deadline or a timeframe to complete those goals.

Before embarking on a new investment, it's important that you know that you are financially capable of doing so. Look at your finances and evaluate them. You have to create a budget and assess and manage your risk by doing your due diligence. Diversifying your portfolio is a way to reduce the risk of your investments, but for that, you need to look at the different types of property you already have in your portfolio and the investments you have in different locations. These are the two most important factors when it comes to diversifying within the real estate industry.

At this point, you have to start thinking strategically in general, but especially when it comes to acquisitions. There are two important things that you need to take into account: either you improve your existing properties or you purchase new investments. Whatever you choose, you should always pay close attention to your finances and how you can cope with the new investments because they might impact your margins and, ultimately, your profits.

But scaling your business doesn't necessarily mean improving existing properties or purchasing new ones. How you manage them is also relevant. If your idea is to manage all your investments, you will have to come up with an efficient management strategy. This could mean purchasing software management tools or hiring a property management company. The first one is recommended if you want to save money, but still want to manage the properties yourself. Hiring a property management company might cost you more, which can ultimately reduce your profits, but you will save more of your time.

Expanding your network and your connections is also part of scaling your business. Attempting to scale on a daily basis can help you build new relationships in the industry, which might lead to new opportunities. In fact, getting into a partnership is a great way to scale your business because you will have a partner who is willing to make a financial effort and help you expand your business. Usually, this means acquiring more properties or helping you financially increase the value of your existing investments. At this point, becoming more tax efficient can really help you maximize your profits.

Even if you're just starting out in this industry, scaling your business should always be the aim. So, you have to make an effort to constantly network with other professionals.

EXPLORING ADVANCED REAL ESTATE STRATEGIES

As you diversify your portfolio and gain more experience, you will inevitably start looking for other strategies that might require a little more knowledge on your part. I'm not going into much detail on any of them, as many require entirely separate books to really know them, but I'll give you the knowledge so that you can dive deeper into them on your own time.

Let's start with commercial real estate. This is not a strategy per se, but when you invest in this type of real estate, it's important that you have acquired some more experience than you had when beginning your real estate investor career. Commercial real estate is a great way to diversify your portfolio, but the approach you have to take is vastly different from, say, residential real estate. Instead of properties where people live, you have to look at office buildings or retail centers, for example. Here, the due diligence you have to do is quite different from that of residential properties, and it's usually more expensive to acquire. On the other hand, it's far more financially stable.

There's also real estate syndication. Here, you pool funds with other like-minded investors, and while this doesn't increase the complexity, there are a few more steps that you have to go through. Also, when doing this, there are usually more properties involved, or at least larger properties, which might contribute to the complexity of the deal. This is especially true when we look at the financial and legal structure of the syndication. Here, it's fairly common to have different types of partners with different powers and functions.

Another more advanced strategy is multifamily real estate. For many real estate investors coming from residential properties, this is the most logical step to follow. Here, you might find apartment complexes that offer multiple income streams. However, the initial investment is often higher than that of single residential properties. There's also more management involved, with more tenant screenings and maintenance.

Tax-related strategies, such as 1031 exchanges that allow you to defer capital gain taxes, are yet another way to dip your toe in more complex real estate strategies. The complexity of these deals often comes from the legal side of things, as, with a 1031 exchange in particular, you have to purchase a property similar to the one you just sold then use the money to purchase the new property, which allows you to defer the capital gained from it. It's important that you work with a tax advisor or an attorney who specializes in these types of deals so you can maximize your profits.

Real estate investment trusts, or REITs, are a simpler but equally successful method. They function similarly to stocks in that they may be bought and sold on the market. However, rather than investing directly in real estate, you are investing in a firm that specializes in real estate property investments. These REIT stocks are structured to provide dividends similar to rental income, giving a consistent income stream, as well as the opportunity for capital development over time. Incorporating REITs into your portfolio is an excellent way to diversify.

Then we have real estate development, which involves buying land and building a property from the ground up. While buying land may be less expensive than buying an existing home, it is important to consider the expenses of hiring workers to complete the building, as well as the time required to finish the project. This approach is more demanding when it comes to due diligence than for already-built properties. It also brings a higher financial commitment.

There are plenty of other advanced strategies, but the ones I've mentioned here are perhaps some of the most common. They are all great ways to get started with these more advanced approaches.

They also tend to lead to higher returns, but they carry more risk than the most basic strategies. You often have to have a completely different understanding of that side of the business, so it's important that you really try to get all the necessary knowledge before pursuing any of these advanced strategies.

Scaling your business is something that should be on your mind—if not now, at least in the future. In this case, it means expanding your portfolio, where you need to set a timeline for when you should advance to expand it, assess your finances to understand if you can do it, and improve your existing properties so you can increase your profit. At the same time, you should continue to expand your professional network to allow you to take advantage of other opportunities.

KEY TAKEAWAYS

- Always be reviewing and checking in with your investment goals.
- Have a team of contractors and repair companies on standby for unexpected problems that arise.
- Make sure you get any necessary permits to renovate your property. This is especially important if you are fixing structural issues.
- It's imperative that you and or your property or project manager stay organized with paperwork, finances, and timelines no matter what strategy you're using.
- Screening tenants is essential to lowering your risk of late rent payment, vacancies, evictions, squatters, or property damage.
- Zillow, Apartments.com, or Realtor.com are great places to find tenants, collect rent, and manage leases.
- Having professional photos and maintaining a seamless application process are key to attracting good tenants.
- Diligently keep records of everything property related for tax and legal reasons.

FREE GIFT #5

The Must-Have Property Rehab Checklist: One mistake can make or break your bank!

Rehabbing a worn-down property is a great way to get a great deal on a property and force its appreciation! Construction also costs time and money which can be a huge money pit if something goes wrong. With this rehab checklist you'll be able to thoroughly understand the process and what things to consider before you start.

To get instant access this free e-book, scan the QR code below or visit this link: www.readstreetpress.com/realestatebonus5

CONCLUSION: YOU CAN DO IT

You are now at the very start of a promising career as a real estate investor, but also at the beginning of achieving your financial freedom, quitting your day job, and especially having the time to do what you love and spend with your loved ones. It won't be easy, especially at the beginning, but you shouldn't be overwhelmed by it.

What you find in this book is everything that you need to know to start. Making changes is the only way we can continue to move forward and achieve things we have never thought of reaching. It's just that first step that we need to make, and from there, we lose the fear of leaving our comfort zone and expand our horizons. There are no more excuses; you know exactly where to start now, and you have the basic knowledge, too. All you have to do now is get out there.

Before I leave you to follow your dreams, I just want to go over the main points we've discussed in this book. However, feel free to peruse those parts you feel you don't fully understand. This is not a one-time read, but a thorough guide to help you navigate the intricacies of real estate investing.

We started by looking at how real estate works, but most importantly, how it can work for you in achieving your goals. We looked at the potential of real estate as a way to build your wealth, how you can maximize your profits through tax, how debt can be leveraged to follow certain opportunities, and how to generate passive income while your investments appreciate. We also looked at the different types of real estate properties you can invest in. The easiest way to get into the industry is to invest in residential properties, but as you gain more experience, commercial properties can be a great way for you to increase your income or even invest in raw land where you have full control of your investment.

Then, we looked at investment strategies and how each presents unique opportunities. Remember, these strategies are not inherently good or bad; it all depends on your situation and how well you can do your due diligence to pick the right one. Then, we moved on to short- and long-term deals, fix-and-flip, and wholesaling. However, everything starts with your very first deal, to which a whole chapter was dedicated. The first deal is often the most important you will make in your career because it will define how you can invest in consequential properties. This is no reason to get overwhelmed by it, though. If you have done your due diligence, understand the market, and have the right people by your side, chances are that everything will go smoothly, and you will be successful.

As we have seen, there are many different steps, such as getting preapproved, creating your budget, and many other things. There will be times when bringing in a partner will make sense. A partner can provide you with enough funds, as well as great insights.

Analyzing deals is perhaps where all the effort lies, but to be very honest, it's my favorite part because I get to understand and be confident about the deals I take on. I went into detail about how you can analyze your deals, but this is something you have to practice, and over time, you will get better at it. Here, you have to go through your due diligence and evaluate the property as well as the market conditions. Once you have all the data, you can make a conscious decision.

The next step is to look for financing, and it's crucial that you know all the different options you can go for. As I've previously said, chances are that traditional financing is the best route when it comes to your first deal. But don't be married to this idea if you are clearly better off with a more creative type of financing, as long as you do your due diligence. Here, finding partners is crucial because they can support you financially, and help when it comes to understanding certain deals.

Once that is all done and decided, it's time to make an offer. At this stage, creating a great offer and knowing how to negotiate can really make your deal successful. But don't forget the closing. Don't think that once the negotiation is done, you are free to do what you want. Your obligations continue, and there's a lot of paperwork involved in closing the deal. This is why you have to work closely with your attorney to make sure everything is in order. After that, you might become a landlord, which often means taking care of maintenance, managing renovations, or screening tenants.

As overwhelming as it might seem, beginnings always feel this way. You have to keep on persevering, and with experience and the confidence you build along the way, things will get easier. And as you continue to move forward in your career, the closer you get to your goal of becoming financially free.

THANK YOU

THANK YOU so much for buy and reading my book! You could have picked from many others, but you chose this one.

Before you go, I want to ask you for one small favor.

 **Can you please leave this book a review on Amazon?**

Leaving a review is the best way to support the work of independent authors like me. You can scan the QR code or visit the link below:

http://amazon.com/review/create-review?&asin=B0CWB5XNT9

Your feedback will help me to keep writing the kind of books that will help you build the real estate empire of your dreams. It would mean a lot to me to hear from you.

 Our mission is to inspire and empower others to break free from the constraints of traditional employment and achieve Permanent PTO through entrepreneurship. We believe everyone can transform their financial future and live the life they've always dreamed of and spend life living.

If you would like more resources, please visit our website: www.permanentpto.com

WOULD YOU LIKE MORE OF OUR BOOKS FOR FREE?

Join Our Exclusive ARC Team—Limited Spots Available!

Do you love being the first to discover groundbreaking books? If so, you're invited to apply for our Advanced Review Copy (ARC) Team!

As a member of this elite group, you'll receive early copies of our upcoming books—completely free. All we ask in return is your honest feedback so we can improve the quality of our content. This is your chance to get exclusive access, influence the book market, and connect with authors and fellow readers.

Why Apply?

- **Early Access:** Be among the first to read and review new titles before they hit the shelves.

- **Influence Others:** Your insights help guide other readers and shape future publications.

- **Exclusive Content:** Get free access to new articles, tools, and more!

Spots are limited to ensure a quality experience for all members. Don't miss this opportunity to make a real impact in the world of real estate and entrepreneurship literature.

Apply online with the QR code or visit https://readstreetpress.com/freebooks to join our ARC Reviewers Team. We look forward to having you!

BIBLIOGRAPHY

Adair, W. P. (n.d.). *William Penn Adair quote.* LinkedIn. https:/ / www.linkedin.com/ pulse/ find-out-where-people-going-buy-land-before-get-william-zahra-ibrahim

Alibhai, E. (2015, November 18). *Find out where the people are going and buy the land before they get there.* Lexology. https:/ / www.lexology.com/ library/ detail.aspx? g=e5404bf2-d33c-43a0-8fb0-02940fbf6c2e

Aston, J. J. (n.d.). Quote. In *20 famous real estate investing quotes.* (n.d.). Realty Mogul. https:/ / www.realtymogul.com/ knowledge-center/ article/ 20-famous-real-estate-investing-quotes#:~:text=% E2% 80% 9CBuy% 20on% 20the% 20fringe% 20and,real% 20estate% 20and% 20business% 20mogul.

Ayers, C. (2023, February 19). *What is the inspection contingency?* Rocket Mortgage. https:/ / www.rocketmortgage.com/ learn/ inspection-contin-gency#:~:text=An% 20inspection% 20contingency% 2C% 20also% 20called

Babaee, A. (2021, December 20). *How to invest in property.* Money. https:/ / www.-money.co.uk/ guides/ how-to-invest-in-property

Barroso, A. & O'Shea, Bev. (2024, January 8). *How to improve credit fast.* Nerdwallet. https:/ / www.nerdwallet.com/ article/ finance/ raise-credit-score-fast

Beattie, A. (2022, July 14). *4 simple ways to invest in real estate.* Investopedia. https:/ / www.investopedia.com/ investing/ simple-ways-invest-real-estate/

Benson, A. (2023, September 12). *Types of real estate investments.* NerdWallet. https:/ / www.nerdwallet.com/ article/ investing/ types-of-real-estate-invest-ments#:~:text=Apartment% 20rentals% 2C% 20REITs% 2C% 20commercial% 20real

Bree, D. (n.d.). *Understanding the different types of real estate loans.* Donn. https:/ / donn.com/ types-of-real-estate-loans/

Burcheri, R. (2023, July 10). *Why investors shouldn't bet their house on real estate investment trusts.* Artemis Funds. https:/ / www.artemisfunds.com/ en/ gbr/ investor/ investment-insights/ 2020/ jul/ why-investors-should-not-bet-house-on-real-estate-investment-trusts

Carnegie, A. *Andrew Carnegie quotes.* AZ Quotes. https:/ / www.azquotes.com/ quote/ 856550

Carson, C. (2021, September 13). *What is creative financing and how to use it in real estate.* Biggerpockets. https:/ / www.biggerpockets.com/ blog/ creative-financing

CFI Team. (2023, January 25). *Price appreciation.* Corporate Finance Institute. https:/ / corporatefinanceinstitute.com/ resources/ valuation/ price-appre-ciation/

Chen, J. (2022, July 6). *Real estate: Definition, types, how to invest in it.* Investopedia. https:/ / www.investopedia.com/ terms/ r/ realestate.asp

DeNicola, L. (2022, June 22). *How to invest in real estate with bad credit.* Experian. https:/ / www.experian.com/ blogs/ ask-experian/ how-to-invest-in-real-estate-with-low-credit/

Eker, T. H. (n.d.). Quote. *In 5 Tips for Winning at Buy and Hold Real Estate Investing* (and *3 Pitfalls to Avoid*). (2023, April 5). Xome. https:/ / www.xome.com/ blog/ 5-tips-for-winning-at-buy-and-hold-real-estate-investing-and-3-pitfalls-to-avoid/

Engel & Völkers Team. (n.d.). *How to build a network in real estate.* Engel & Völkers. https:/ / www.engelvoelkers.com/ en/ blog/ company/ job-career/ how-to-build-a-network-in-real-estate/

Experian Team. (n.d.). *How to improve your credit score.* Experian. https:/ / www.experian.com/ blogs/ ask-experian/ credit-education/ improving-credit/ improve-credit-score/

First Webers Realtors Team. (2017, September 25). *Invest in yourself! "Real estate provides the highest returns, the greatest values and the least risk."* Firstweber. https:/ / blog.firstweber.com/ 2017/ 09/ 25/ invest-in-yourself-real-estate-provides-the-highest-returns-the-greatest-values-and-the-least-risk/

G. Wright, R. (2021, March 29). *5 tips to making an offer on an investment property.* The Investors Edge. https:/ / www.theinvestorsedge.com/ blog/ 5-tips-to-making-an-offer-on-an-investment-property

Gariepy, L. (2023, January 12). *Top 6 tax benefits of real estate investing.* Rocket Mortgage. https:/ / www.rocketmortgage.com/ learn/ tax-benefits-of-real-estate-investing

Gilbert, A. (2016, April 8). *Top 8 property investment strategies.* Progressive Property. https:/ / www.progressiveproperty.co.uk/ property-investment-strategies/

Kagan, J. (2021, February 25). *Mortgage.* Investopedia. https:/ / www.investopedia.com/ terms/ m/ mortgage.asp

Kilroy, A. (2023, June 7). *A guide to closing documents for buyers.* Rocket Mortgage. https:/ / www.rocketmortgage.com/ learn/ closing-documents

Lerner, M. (2023, May 19). *5 things you need to be pre-approved for a mortgage.* Investopedia. https:/ / www.investopedia.com/ financial-edge/ 0411/ 5-things-you-need-to-be-pre-approved-for-a-mortgage.aspx#:~:text=Pre% 2Dapproval% 20requires% 20proof% 20of

Ligon, M. (2023, September 14). *Council post: A step-by-step guide to analyzing real estate investment deals.* Forbes. https:/ / www.forbes.com/ sites/ forbesbusiness-council/ 2023/ 09/ 14/ a-step-by-step-guide-to-analyzing-real-estate-invest-ment-deals/ ?sh=236d085f7d7d

Nguyen, J. (2021, December 5). *4 key factors that drive the real estate market.* Investopedia. https:/ / www.investopedia.com/ articles/ mortages-real-estate/ 11/ factors-affecting-real-estate-market.asp

Pomroy, K. (2022, November 4). *What is the due diligence period in real estate?* Experian. https:/ / www.experian.com/ blogs/ ask-experian/ what-is-due-diligence-period-real-estate/

Prater, M. (2023, October 2). *34 motivational, relatable, & funny real estate quotes every agent should read.* Blog.hubspot.com. https:/ / blog.hubspot.com/ sales/ real-estate-quotes

Real Estate Investor Goddesses Team. (2021, April 26). *7 reasons why 90% of million-aires are invested in real estate.* Real Estate Investor Goddesses. https:/ / www.realestateinvestorgoddesses.com/ blog/ 7-reasons-you-should-be-investing-in-real-estate

RealtyMoguls Team. (n.d.). *20 famous real estate investing quotes.* Realty Mogul. https:/ / www.realtymogul.com/ knowledge-center/ article/ 20-famous-real-estate-investing-quotes

RealVantage Team. (2020, November 21). *15 famous real estate investment quotes / realvantage insights*. Real Insights. https:/ / www.realvantage.co/ insights/ 15-famous-real-estate-investment-quotes/

Rockefeller, J. D. (n.d.). *John D. Rockefeller quote*. AZ Quotes. https:/ / www.azquotes.com/ quote/ 814175

Rohde, J. (2022, December 12). *How to make a successful offer on a property in 7 steps*. Roofstock. https:/ / learn.roofstock.com/ blog/ how-to-make-an-offer-on-a-property

Roosevelt, F. D. (n.d.). *Franklin D. Roosevelt quotes*. AZ Quotes. https:/ / www.azquotes.com/ quote/ 628914

Sage, R. (n.d.). Quote. In *15 famous real estate investment quotes*. (2020, November 21). Real Vantage Insights. https:/ / www.realvantage.co/ insights/ 15-famous-real-estate-investment-quotes/

Segal, T. (2019). *Federal housing administration loan – FHA loan – definition*. Investopedia. https:/ / www.investopedia.com/ terms/ f/ fhaloan.asp

Seth, S. (2021, December 9). *13 steps of a real estate closing*. Investopedia. https:/ / www.investopedia.com/ articles/ mortgages-real-estate/ 10/ closing-home-process.asp

Smith, L. (2023, August 17). *Leverage: Increasing your real estate net worth*. Investopedia. https:/ / www.investopedia.com/ articles/ mortgages-real-estate/ 10/ increase-your-real-estate-net-worth.asp#:~:text=Leverage% 20uses% 20borrowed% 20capital% 20or

Stanger, T. (2019, April 25). *What's a good credit score?* Consumer Reports. https:/ / www.consumerreports.org/ banking-credit/ what-is-a-good-credit-score/

St. Onge, P. (2015, September 14). *The fallacy of "buy land — they're not making anymore."* Mises Institute. https:/ / mises.org/ library/ fallacy-buy-land-theyre-not-making-any-more

Twain, M. (n.d.). *Mark Twain quotes*. Brainy Quotes. https:/ / www.brainyquote.com/ quotes/ mark_twain_380355

Wang, V. (n.d.). *What is real estate and how does it work?* UpNest. https:/ / www.up-nest.com/ 1/ post/ what-is-real-estate-and-how-does-it-work/

Waronker, D. (n.d.). Quote. In Krosman, K. (n.d.). *99 famous real estate quotes and sayings*. Placester. https:/ / placester.com/ real-estate-marketing-academy/ famous-real-estate-quotes-and-sayings

Williams, A. (n.d.). *Armstrong Williams quote*. Brainy Quote. https:/ / www.brainyquote.com/ quotes/ armstrong_williams_291565

Made in the USA
Coppell, TX
15 July 2024

34603537R00090